"Wow! Moving stories, po   1
truths. *Hold Fast* helps u. ⎯⎯⎯⎯⎯⎯ ⎯⎯⎯⎯ ⎯⎯⎯⎯⎯⎯ we face
to fully embrace God's call on our life. Read it, enjoy it, let it sink
down deep. Get in touch with what is keeping you from living a life
abandoned to the person and purposes of Jesus Christ."

— Steve Shadrach, Director of Center for Mission Mobilization,
Author of *The Fuel and the Flame* and *The God Ask*

"Josh's years of experience working with students is on full display,
using powerful and relevant illustrations that cut straight to the issues
facing the next generation of student missionaries. A simple read
that has deep and complex implications for every person considering
God's call to the nations."

— Jason Wu, OMF International

"Clear and compelling! Josh is articulate in person and this comes
through brilliantly in this book. Every Christian college student
should read this! Imagine a generation that takes God's missional
vision seriously and stops making excuses."

— Pete Errington, Director of Recruiting at
Mission to Unreached Peoples

"Josh's service to readers is that he doesn't try to conquer our obstacles
by minimizing them, but gets down to how real and significant they
really are and then throws light on how they may be overcome! His
illustrations and use of Scripture give hope-filled direction to all of
us stumbling down bouldered pathways to follow Jesus —this will be
my go-to when counseling people who are developing a missional
lifestyle."

— Courtney Faulk, Café 1040

"Josh does a fantastic job of helping me better understand God's heart for the nations, and how we can be a part of His master plan. As someone who sends university students around the world, I am recommending this to anyone interested in going to the world. Whether you desire to be involved in reaching the nations through prayer, sending your own teams, or going yourself, this is a must read."

— Shane Sebastian, CRU Global Missions, National Director

"Landmines. Pitfalls. Detours. The mission road is littered with wanna-be missionaries who were not skilled or coached to avoid them. Whether you are a go-er taking first steps toward the nations, or a stayer tasked with coaching missionary candidates, Josh's book will be your wise and encouraging travel guide."

— Matt Burns, Perspectives on the World Christian Movement Global, Managing Director

"Some books you read for fun, others you read out of interest, and then there are some you read for others. The world needs you to read this book. And don't merely read it, respond to it."

— Andrew Knight, Campus Outreach, North Area Director

HOLD FAST

The Mission of God
& the Obstacles of Man

JOSH COOPER

BookVillages

To my parents,
for showing me what it means to
Hold Fast to Jesus.

Contents

Foreword

Following God and pursuing His heart for the nations is an incredible privilege, no matter what service or location that means. I've even heard it said that if God calls you to be a missionary, you shouldn't stoop to be a king. Indeed, what could be greater than partnering with God in His promised-to-succeed plan of reaching all nations? Nothing! How glorious to someday see disciples of Christ in all corners of the earth. The thought is overwhelming.

Yet, when such an opportunity arises, so many of us whimper, complain, fight, and even *run* from it. Jesus tells a parable about a man who sent an invitation to attend a lavish dinner. What an honor! And yet Luke records the response of everyone on the guest list: "But they all alike began to make excuses" (Luke 14:18).

We too are quick to overlook the compliment of being invited to serve God while we focus on the personal sacrifice or inconvenience. I've seen it personally on countless occasions. Excuses and obstacles abound. From within—feelings of inadequacy, doubt, fear, the bondage of sin, misplaced priorities, and potential failure hold us back from following God unreservedly. From without—our friends, children, parents, and even our own spouses can hinder us from moving forward. In my own personal experience, a Christian never graduates from the temptation to let these obstacles have the louder voice. While I believe this experience—this following God and wrestling with excuses—to be universal among Christians, we rarely admit our struggle. This is why I so appreciate Josh's transparent and very honest approach in *Hold Fast*.

I first met Josh when he was a college student. Early on I sensed a deep commitment to following God no matter what. As you will soon discover throughout the pages of this down-to-earth book, Josh is an individual who is not just discussing the issues and obstacles we face but is confronting them in his own life as well. This has been true as long as I have known him. He has wisdom beyond his years, and it is evident in his speaking and writing. You hold in your hand something far beyond a list of barriers. This is a road map of how to navigate around and through them. Chapter by chapter, page by page, you will see yourself in *Hold Fast*. You will come away from this book more encouraged, confident, and equipped to follow God in the calling He has for you. The real joy is in surrendering your excuses and accepting the privilege of following God wherever He may lead you. Josh's book will help you get there.

Dr. Todd Ahrend
International Director, The Traveling Team
Author of *In This Generation* and *The Abrahamic Revolution*

Acknowledgments

I saac Newton once said, "If I have seen further than others, it is by standing on the shoulders of giants." Throughout my life, I've not only stood next to giants, but they have actually hoisted me up. It's time to pause and say thanks to them.

I first thank my support team. They are the foundation of my ministry. Though they are giants, they have gone to their knees for me. Thank you for your prayer and support.

I think of The Traveling Team. My coworkers. They have refined me by their wisdom and faithfulness to Christ. Thank you, Claude Hickman, for your leadership and direction.

I think of Dr. John Piper. Rare is the man who preaches the gospel and God's mission from the pulpit. If books are absent teachers, Dr. Piper has been my personal tutor since I trusted in Christ.

I think of Will. You showed me what it means to be a giant for the unreached. Jonathan, you exemplify by putting your hand to the plow and not looking back. Hudson, you are a humble giant in fellowship and prayer. Dr. John Marc, you epitomize what it means to be a friend.

And to the giant who taught me to speak, write, mobilize, and laugh, Todd Ahrend. I've learned more from you than I can express. Your influence permeates every page of this book and every step of my life.

And to my family. My anchor. Kevin, the living example of enjoying Christ. Danna, you have always been my number one cheerleader. And until my final breath, I will continually discover the depth of the blessing my parents have been to me. I love you dearly.

"If you want to build a ship, don't drum up people to collect wood and don't assign them tasks and work, but rather teach them to long for the endless immensity of the sea."

ANTOINE DE SAINT-EXUPÉRY

Chapter One

Hold Fast

The Challenge

G rande two-thirds decaf, nonfat, no-whip, upside-down, extra-hot, double-shot cinnamon dolce latte, for here ... This is my normal order at a coffee shop these days. I am not at all unusual. I've heard longer. This drink is more than a drink; it is a barometer of our culture. At Starbucks there are 19,000 options.[1] Americans are smothered by choice. This abundance of possibilities has typically been viewed as a great thing that makes life more enjoyable and more palatable. However, with more options come more decisions. With more decisions comes confusion on which way to take.

Growing up, I had one passion: sports. I always knew my life was going to revolve around it. When I got to high school I started wondering how my sports passion would play into my degree. I finally found my answer: biomedical engineering. That's right. Engineering. My thought process was straightforward and simple. If I could get a degree in science, a job with a medical company, I could then be a sales-rep so I could play golf with clients all day long. My salary would be determined by my golf swing. My dreams finally became reality. Until I got to college.

My first semester, I met a guy who was sharing the gospel in my dorm. He knocked on my door and shared Christ with me. Within minutes I understood an illustration that summed up the main theme of the Bible. His parting words for me were, "It sounds like you know a lot about the gospel. What are you doing about it?" That dug into my soul for the next six months. As he continued to come around, we studied the Bible, went to the gym, and even began to share the gospel together. At the time it felt like we were just hanging out; in reality he was investing in me. He started showing me God's passion through the Bible. He pointed out to me that God's heart is to redeem people from every tribe, tongue, and nation. He showed me that as a believer I had a role to play in missions, and it caused me to ask the question, "What am I doing with my life?"

But go? Me? No way. I would be forgotten. I would be miserable. I would be without my comforts. I didn't want to die single. It was one thing to hear about missions. It was another to do it. The distance between God's desire and mine were miles apart.

Jesus told a parable about a man who threw a great banquet. He sent his servant to gather those who had been invited. "But they all began making excuses" (Luke 14:18, NLT). The first said he needed to manage his field, the second needed to tend to his oxen, and the third was newly married. These weren't just any excuses. Under Jewish law, some of these exempted people from war duty (see Deuteronomy 20:1-8). The guests were using good excuses, just in the wrong context. The banquet was meant as a celebration, yet no one wanted to come. The man responded by extending the invitation to others. He was determined to host the celebration regardless of the initial response. Excuses won't stop the party.

THE OBSTACLES

I have traveled the country speaking and meeting with college students from over 150 colleges, teaching God's heart for the world and challenging people to live missionally. Recently, at a university in Georgia, I met with three guys who desired to live in radical obedience to God. Going wherever. Doing whatever. Except there was a problem. Well, three to be exact.

Steve, a sophomore, said he had been on a few short-term trips and was looking toward full-time ministry. Despite his passion, one thing seemed to keep coming up: funding. I asked him about his view of support raising. Asking people for money was excruciating for Steve. He couldn't imagine doing it full-time. He was torn between money and missions. His obstacle: *Money was standing in the way of a passionate laborer and the nations.*

Sitting next to Steve was a freshman named Eric. Eric grew up in a wealthy family. He was fired up about sharing Christ in war-torn territories. He knew that if the gospel was going to these areas, he would be the one to lead the way. As the conversation continued he shared that his parents had a different plan for him. He was torn between obeying God and honoring his parents. His obstacle: *Christian parents were standing in the way of a passionate laborer and the nations.*

And then there was Mark. He was torn between his heart for ministry and his girlfriend's refusal of it. What would happen if they married? He had to choose between God and a girl. His obstacle: *A girl was standing in the way of a passionate laborer and the nations.*

The excuses are real. Everyone has at least one *good* reason why they shouldn't live their life for the mission of God. Therefore, most people who live for God's purpose won't end up doing so accidentally. Out of the hundreds of thousands challenged to be missional Christians, only a small handful make it.

Most obstacles keeping you from living a missional lifestyle are not bad things. Yet, living in obedience means saying no to many good opportunities. We must identify and understand the obstacles and learn how to navigate them on our journey. Whether a doctor, teacher, engineer, pastor, lawyer, or wedding planner, everyone can live their life for the glory of God among all nations.

I have discussed the missional lifestyle with hundreds of young adults. In those conversations, I have listened to dozens of doubts. Unquestionably, nine obstacles consistently emerge: the unknown commission, needs at home, materialism, relationships, family, theology, calling, debt, and support raising.

We all play a role in God's mission. It's not just an option. Deep down, we all desire to live life with maximum impact in obedience to God. Yet, somehow and somewhere, many fall off. Why? How?

Following Christ requires persistence, and nothing rings truer than the words from Scripture, "Hold fast to the hope set before us" (Hebrews 6:18, ESV). "Hold fast" is a phrase rooted in sailing. Ships were covered with ropes. In the midst of an emergency, the captain would shout the order "Hold fast!" to the entire crew. This meant to stop all they were doing and secure the loose rope. By "holding fast" the ropes, the crew was able to keep the ship on course through the most extreme conditions. The writer of Hebrews tells us to hold fast to the hope given by God, to be encouraged to persevere in obedience to Him. Storms and troubles are a reality for both boats and life. We are called to weather the troubles and sail the ocean.

There is a charted course for each of us. We will find hope in the obstacles of life and see God's North Star so we can navigate through. We can overcome. Journey with me as we embark on the mission of God and *hold fast* through the obstacles of man.

ENDNOTES

1. Paul Borthwick, *Simplify* (Colorado Springs, CO: Authentic Publishing, 2007), 8.

Chapter Two

Every Tribe, Tongue, and Nation
Unknown Commission

My college roommate was a very smart guy. His first two years of college were loaded with classes I couldn't even pronounce. By his junior year, he wanted an easy A. He went to the university's list of courses and tried to find the simplest class the university offered. After a few hours of searching, he found it: judo. Why was it so easy? All you had to do was show up. But guess what? He failed. The easiest class on campus, and he failed it. How could this happen? Simple. He forgot he was enrolled in the class. Each day, the judo instructor was marking my roommate absent until he failed the class. It's the only F on his transcript. Who knew you can fail a class even if you don't know you're enrolled?

As believers God has enrolled us in a mission. We all participate in bringing about the purpose of God. This is what God has been pursuing since the beginning of time. For believers, this is not an elective. As I meet Christians across the country, the sad reality is most never show up for the most important course of their life. Why? They never know they're enrolled. It's our *unknown* excuse. Did you realize you were made for a purpose? Many are coasting through life unaware God has a mission and has invited them to join. So each day, they are being marked absent from the purpose they were made for.

In the history of sailing, ships were deployed by some of the world's most powerful kings. Longing to conquer new areas, sailors would set sail with an order from their king to explore the open seas. For believers, God is the owner of our ship, and His mission *is* His order to us. When we understand the King's orders, we will have direction for our journey. We will know the purpose we were made for and how we are to chart the course. By aligning our purposes with God's, we can joyfully let go of other things and hold fast to the promises of God. But what are these orders? What exactly is God's purpose?

From Genesis to Revelation, God has laid out His mission. He has shown us His desire for every believer. Ask yourself, "Do I know God's mission?" Let's trace this purpose God has laid out through Scripture. If this is what God is doing, we need to know what it is. Let's take a step back and look at a panoramic view of the Bible, from beginning to end.

THE BEGINNING

In the beginning God created man and woman to worship and fellowship with Him. God gave them a specific command: "Be fruitful and multiply and fill the earth" (Genesis 1:28, ESV). Though a physical command, there were spiritual intentions. God wants people from every tribe, tongue, and nation to worship Him. Can you imagine the whole earth filled with worshippers of God?

By chapter 3 of Genesis man had sinned and communion with God was broken. In chapter 6 Scripture says that "every intention of the thoughts of his heart was only evil continually" (Genesis 6:5, ESV). God flooded the earth and started over with Noah. God said to Noah, "Be fruitful and multiply and fill the earth" (9:1, ESV). That sounds familiar. For a second time God gives the command to fill the earth. This time it works, sort of ...

Now the whole world had one language and a common
speech. As people moved eastward, they found a plain in
Shinar and settled there....

Then they said, "Come, let us build ourselves a city,
with a tower that reaches to the heavens, so that we may
make a name for ourselves; otherwise we will be scattered
over the face of the whole earth." (Genesis 11:1-2,4)

Humanity started to spread out, but found a town, Shinar,
and decided to construct a tower. Not at all what God had said
to do. This is direct disobedience. God commanded to "fill the
earth," and man said "no thanks."

What did God do next? He said:

"Come, let us go down and confuse their language so
they will not understand each other." So the LORD
scattered them from there over all the earth, and they
stopped building the city. (vv. 7-8)

They didn't obey, so God intervened. Confusing their
language, He scattered them. We went from one language to
many. With multiple languages came multiple difficulties. But
God had a plan to fill the earth with worshippers. He looked
down and used one man to reach all people on earth—the man
we know as Abraham, the idol worshipper from modern-day
Iraq.[1]

The LORD had said to Abram, "Go from your country,
your people and your father's household to the land I will
show you.
I will make you into a great nation,
and I will bless you;

I will make your name great,
and you will be a blessing.
I will bless those who bless you,
and whoever curses you I will curse;
and all peoples on earth
will be blessed through you. (12:1-3)

God commanded Abram to leave the things he knew for a place He would show him. God didn't tell him where. He simply said, "leave." The next verse reads, "So Abram went, as the LORD had told him" (12:4). Abram was seventy-five. The old man didn't object. He didn't delay. He simply left. This has been called the Abrahamic Revolution.[2] It's the point in someone's life when they decide to give up everything to follow after God, no matter where He leads them. This is a pivotal moment in Scripture. Abraham not only trusted God for his afterlife but with his present life. He was sailing into the open waters of life with no land in sight. Abraham held fast to God for his provision. In obedience, he moved from his homeland and followed the Lord, because Abraham received a promise showing him this blessing was bigger than his life. It was for *all peoples on earth.*

Abraham wasn't the only one who received this blessing. God also gave it to Abraham's son Isaac:

I will be with you and will bless you ... and I will establish the oath that I swore to Abraham your father. I will multiply your offspring as the stars of heaven and will give to your offspring all these lands. And in your offspring all the nations of the earth shall be blessed. (Genesis 26:3-4, ESV)

And to Isaac's son Jacob:

> Your descendants will be like the dust of the earth, and
> you will spread out to the west and to the east, to the
> north and to the south. All peoples on earth will be
> blessed through you and your offspring. (Genesis 28:14)

Jacob was renamed Israel, and his descendants became known as the nation of Israel. God remembered His promise to Jacob and blessed the nation of Israel so that all peoples on earth would be blessed. God blessed Israel to bless the nations. From the first book of the Bible God has one mission: all nations.

THE STORIES OF HIS GLORY

Throughout the Old Testament, God's purpose is to show His glory to the nations. Think of the exodus of Israel from Egypt. Scripture says, "And I will gain glory through Pharaoh and all his army, through his chariots and his horsemen. The Egyptians will know that I am the LORD" (Exodus 14:17-18). God miraculously freed the Israelites *from* the Egyptians to make His glory known *to* the Egyptians. Yet, the Exodus wasn't just for Israel, and it wasn't just for the Egyptians. As God delivered the Israelites by splitting the waters and allowing them to cross the Red Sea on dry land, He was establishing His reputation. Years later Rahab would say,

> We have heard how the LORD dried up the water of the
> Red Sea for you when you came out of Egypt.... When we
> heard of it, our hearts melted in fear and everyone's cour-
> age failed because of you, for the LORD your God is God in
> heaven above and on the earth below. (Joshua 2:10-11)

God delivered Israel, and decades later other nations were still talking about the one true, living God in Israel.

The same story occurred with the inhabitants of Gibeon, the Hivites. In the book of Joshua, the Hivites recounted the miracle of God delivering the Israelites: "For we have heard reports of him: all that he did in Egypt" (9:9). God was using Israel as a light to lead the nations to Himself.

Consider David and Goliath. This classic story is a great inspiration, but there was something bigger happening. The giant foreigner, Goliath, was mocking the God of Israel, and David shouted to him, "This day the LORD will deliver you into my hands, and I'll strike you down…. And the whole world will know that there is a God in Israel" (1 Samuel 17:46). This story is larger than David and Goliath. Larger than Israel. God used David as a megaphone to the nations.

Other stories that display the glory of God for the world are Shadrach, Meshach, and Abednego (see Daniel 3:28-30), Daniel and the lions' den (see Daniel 6:25-27), Solomon's wisdom (see 1 Kings 10:24), the temple and the foreigner (see 2 Chronicles 6:32-33), and Nehemiah and the walls of Jerusalem (see Nehemiah 6:15-16).

As we move through the Old Testament into the Psalms, one cannot escape our global God. The psalmists said:

> Let all the earth fear the LORD; let all the people of the world revere him. (33:8)

> All the nations you have made will come and worship before you, Lord; they will bring glory to your name.
> For you are great and do marvelous deeds; you alone are God. (86:9-10)

Declare his glory among the nations, his marvel⟨
among all peoples. For great is the LORD and mo⟨
of praise; he is to be feared above all gods. (96:3⟨

Praise the LORD, all you nations; extol him, all you
peoples. (117:1)

The Lord raised up prophets to remind Israel of their
purpose. Through Isaiah He said, "It is too small a thing for
you to be my servant to restore the tribes of Jacob and bring
back those of Israel I have kept. I will also make you a light
for the Gentiles, that my salvation may reach to the ends of
the earth" (Isaiah 49:6). Through the prophet Ezekiel He said,
"The nations will know that I am the LORD ... when through
you I vindicate my holiness" (Ezekiel 36:23, ESV). Repeatedly,
the prophets resounded the Lord's fame to the nations:

The LORD will be awesome to them when he destroys all
the gods of the earth. Distant nations will bow down to
him, all of them in their own lands. (Zephaniah 2:11)

"I will shake all nations, and what is desired by all
nations will come, and I will fill this house with glory,"
says the LORD Almighty. (Haggai 2:7)

And the LORD will be king over all the earth. On that
day there will be one LORD—his name alone will be
worshiped. (Zechariah 14:9, NLT)

My name will be great among the nations, from where
the sun rises to where it sets. In every place incense and
pure offerings will be brought to me, because my name
will be great among the nations. (Malachi 1:11)

,SUS AND THOSE WHO FOLLOW

In the Old Testament God created the human race, distinguished the nation of Israel as His own, and displayed His glory to the nations through Israel. As the Old Testament comes to a close Israel is still waiting for the fulfillment of the promise given to Abraham. From the first verse of the New Testament, we can see Jesus' life and ministry are focused on bringing glory to the Father. He was able to fulfill the promise of blessing all peoples on earth, because He is in the lineage of Abraham. The New Testament begins with the words "This is the genealogy of Jesus the Messiah the son of David, the son of Abraham" (Matthew 1:1). What God promised to Abraham, Jesus fulfills.

In His birth, Jesus is a testimony to the nations. Wise men from *countries in the east* came to glorify the newborn Lord (see Matthew 2:11), and an angel told the shepherds that Jesus' birth was great news for *all people* (see Luke 2:10).[3] At Jesus' dedication, Simeon blessed Him, saying, "My eyes have seen your salvation, which you have prepared in the sight of all nations: a light for revelation to the Gentiles, and the glory of your people Israel" (2:30-32). The life of Christ would indeed be much bigger than Israel ever imagined.

In the Old Testament, God chose the Jewish people to display His glory to the world. Throughout their history, the Jews anticipated a powerful king who would redeem the nation of Israel. In the first century AD, the Jews saw only two people groups: themselves and anyone not Jewish—the Gentiles. Gentiles didn't keep the Jewish laws, so the Jews viewed them as unclean and unworthy. Associating with a Gentile was not only frowned upon but would make a Jewish person unclean.

As a religious leader, Jesus pushed the cultural boundaries. The majority of Jesus' miracles were done for Gentiles. Take, for example, the feeding of the four thousand (see Mark 8), the healing of the Canaanite's daughter (see Matthew 15:21-28), the Samaritan at the well (see John 4), and the healing of the demon-possessed Gadarene men (see Matthew 8:28-34). All these miracles were to show God's love is not just for the people of Israel, but for all nations.

Jesus' actions as well as His teachings reflected the heart of God for all nations. In Matthew 24 Jesus' disciples were curious about the end of the Jewish captivity and the beginning of the Messiah's reign. They asked Jesus, "Tell us, ... when will this happen, and what will be the sign of your coming and of the end of the age?" (v. 3). His response included wars, famines, earthquakes, and lawlessness. He continued, "This gospel of the kingdom will be preached in the whole world as a testimony to all nations, and then the end will come" (v. 14). From the lips of the Savior came the promise of the fulfillment of the glory of God reaching the ends of the earth.

Jesus concluded His ministry by giving five commissionings. Each commission is a powerful proclamation declaring what His followers should be about:

> All authority in heaven and on earth has been given to me. Therefore go and make disciples of all nations. (Matthew 28:18-19)

> Go into all the world and preach the gospel to all creation. (Mark 16:15)

> Repentance for the forgiveness of sins will be preached in his name to all nations. (Luke 24:47)

> As the Father has sent me, I am sending you. (John 20:21)

> You will be my witnesses in Jerusalem, and in all Judea
> and Samaria, and to the ends of the earth. (Acts 1:8)

One could paraphrase Jesus' words, "Disciples, don't forget. We're not done. I've got to go, but it doesn't stop here. It doesn't stop with you. It's going to the nations."

Paul, one of the greatest missionaries in history, said it was his life goal to glorify God among the nations. "I make it my ambition to preach the gospel, not where Christ has already been named, lest I build on someone else's foundation" (Romans 15:20, ESV). He went to the places in his world where the gospel wasn't, because that is where the gospel was needed. Deep down inside of us there should be something that wants to echo that statement Paul made in Romans 15:20.[4] Paul had a pioneering spirit, not because of his personality but because he saw Jesus as worthy to receive glory from those in Israel and beyond.

The promise given to Abraham that through his offspring *all nations would be blessed* came as the gospel in Jesus Christ. Through His perfect life and His atoning death and resurrection God has made a way by faith for us to be brought to glorious communion with Him. In Galatians, Paul showed that we are the connection of the gospel to the nations. "If you are Christ's, then you are Abraham's offspring, heirs according to promise" (Galatians 3:29, ESV). Paul said as Christians, we have been grafted into Abraham's family. We have received the same promise as Abraham, Isaac, and Jacob to bless all peoples on earth. We were made for this!

In Revelation, we see a foretaste of this promise kept when John gets a glimpse of heaven:

> After this I looked, and behold, a great multitude that

no one could number, from every nation, from all tribes
and peoples and languages, standing before the throne
and before the Lamb, clothed in white robes, with palm
branches in their hands, and crying out with a loud
voice, "Salvation belongs to our God who sits on the
throne, and to the Lamb!" (Revelation 7:9-10, ESV)

God reveals to us there will be people from every tribe, tongue, and nation standing before the throne worshipping the Lamb who was slain. Heaven will be one massive, multicultural worship service. People from every people group will be worshipping Jesus. This is a promise. It will happen. Just like Abraham, Moses, David, Solomon, and the faithful people in history who have stepped out in faith to see this fulfilled, so will we. God said it would happen. He will accomplish it! We should hold fast to His promise.

The Bible isn't sixty-six individual books. It is one book with one theme. From beginning to end God reveals His desire of being known and exalted in every corner of the earth. This is the story of God's glory and our purpose. Each believer is responsible to act, think, pray, and live for the glory of God among the nations. He has sent us as sailors to extend the dominion of His kingdom to the places it isn't. Our role as believers is to be conduits of God's grace, and our motivation is the glory of God in the salvation of His people.

Today the rallying cry has not changed. Unfortunately, the glimpse of eternity John gave in Revelation 7:9 is not the way the world looks yet. There are still millions of people without access to the gospel.

On January 1, 1863, Abraham Lincoln issued an order that has impacted the world to this day. He signed the Emancipation Proclamation, proclaiming freedom for America's slaves. On that day up to fifty thousand people who were once bound in shackles of slavery were given freedom. These men, women, and children saw freedom for the first time in their lives. What an incredible gift. Sadly, at that time in the United States there were four million slaves. If you had traveled south to a Georgia plantation, walked up to a slave, and asked him about the Emancipation Proclamation, he may not even have known what you were talking about! One slave stated, "I don't know nothing bout Abraham Lincoln ... cep they say he sot us free. And I don't know nothing bout that neither."[5] He may have *heard* of the Civil War, or Abraham Lincoln, or slaves being freed, but the reality was that every day he, his wife, and his child would still wake up, work the fields all day long, and go to bed as slaves. He would know nothing of freedom until Union troops arrived to advance the order.

Likewise, two thousand years ago Jesus Christ died proclaiming good news to slaves and freedom to captives. With His blood He purchased people from every people group. Yet today, there are two billion people living without access to the gospel. They will never hear about Jesus, never see a Bible, and most will never meet a Christian. They will never rejoice in the one thing that can save their souls. God is inviting us to get involved with what He is doing. The only thing standing between us and them is our obstacles. The question is, will we hold fast?

ENDNOTES

1. Joshua 24:2; Genesis 11:26-28.
2. Todd Ahrend, *The Abrahamic Revolution* (Colorado Springs, CO: NavPress, 2011).

3. Matthew 2:1 says the Magi were from "the east," implying they were from other nations. Luke 2:10 says Jesus' birth is great news for "all people" because Jesus came to purchase people from every people group (Revelation 5:9).

4. Missions mobilizer Hudson Smith first challenged me with this quote.

5. Shelby Foote, *The Civil War: A Narrative: Volume 3: Red River to Appomattox* (New York, Vantage Books, 1986), quoted in Charles Swindoll, *The Grace Awakening* (Nashville, TN: Thomas Nelson, 2003), 95.

Chapter Three

Another Man's Foundation

Needs At Home

Matthew Emmons was one of America's greatest competition rifle shooters. From the Junior Olympics forward Emmons set the pace in the sport of rifle shooting. Other competitors set their sights on Emmons; if they were going to get the gold, they had to outshoot him. They would try anything. In the 2004 US Olympic preliminaries, Emmons discovered his rifle had been sabotaged with a screwdriver. With a borrowed gun, he went on to earn a spot on the US team. At the Olympic games in Athens, Emmons focused on a target the size of a dime from over half a football field away. He hit it fifty-nine out of sixty times, sending him into the final round, Emmons on top, everyone else chasing.[1] He was on track to make history. All he had to do was hit one final shot to win the gold. Emmons did the same thing he did every time: stepped up, stared down the scope, released the safety, took a deep breath, calmed his nerves, pulled the trigger, and nailed the bull's-eye. However, there was a problem: no buzzer registered the hit. He lowered the gun and signaled to the referees. There must have been a mistake. Then he heard the news: he had zeroed in on the wrong target. He shot one lane over. With one shot, Matthew Emmons dropped from first to eighth. He had the gold medal in his reach, yet shot the wrong target.

How many Christians set their sights on a target only to realize at the end of their life they are pursuing the wrong one— aligning their life one lane over? It can be easy to set our life toward the wrong goal. We wrongly target our desires instead of God's.

While I was sitting at a Starbucks in Texas one day, I realized a guy kept looking at me. I wondered if I knew him, but I didn't. Eventually, he stood up and started over toward me. He said, "Are you reading your Bible?" "Yeah," I replied. "How exciting," he responded. "There are virtually no Christians here." I have to admit, I was caught off guard. I had been in the city only a few days, met many believers, saw dozens of churches, and I wasn't even the only one in the coffee shop reading my Bible! I honestly didn't know how to feel. Was he disconnected? Was he confused?

Each of us can walk down our city street and see the need for more Christian laborers. We need help with the poor, help in youth ministry and college ministry. There are needs everywhere. However, the question to direct our focus should not be "Where are the needs?" The question is "Where are the *greatest* needs?"

Five years ago, I hardly knew other religions existed. I couldn't tell you the difference between a Native American Indian and an Indian from India. My thoughts of Muslims didn't go beyond the association with terrorists. As I learned through Scripture about God's passion, I started understanding how He sees the world. That changed the way I saw it. I realized my definition of missions needed to align with God's. In Revelation 5:9 God gives us His definition of missions: "And they sang a new song, saying: 'You are worthy to take the scroll and to open its seals, because you were slain, and with your blood you purchased for God persons *from every tribe and language and people and nation.*'" God's ultimate goal in the Bible and all of history is to be known and worshipped by every nation, tribe, people, and language. Missions is extending worship where worship isn't. If this is His ultimate goal, it must be ours. All our resources need to be applied to seeing this become a reality. Yet many will not live, think, and act missionally because "local needs" trump "greatest needs."

WHAT'S A NATION?
In Matthew 28:19 Jesus commissioned His followers to "make disciples of all nations." He used the Greek word *ethnos*, which means "nations." Today when we use the word "nation," we think geopolitical boundaries, like Iran or China. However, the way Christ used it was completely different. Though translated as "nations," it should be understood as "race or tribes." This is where we get the terms "ethnic groups" or "people groups." A people group is best described as an ethnolinguistic group, meaning people who look alike, act alike, and speak the same language. It is the furthest the gospel can spread within a group without hitting a significant barrier.[2]

If we sent missionary teams to Nigeria and saw people respond to Christ, churches established, and disciples made, this would be considered a success. Would this be enough? Not if the missionaries were all going to the same people group. According to Joshua Project, Nigeria is composed of 524 people groups with 508 different languages. We must not be consumed with *where* we are sending missionaries but *to whom* we are sending them. We must think in terms of people groups, not countries.

There are approximately 17,000 people groups in the world today.[3] Of these people groups, nearly 7,000 are without access to the gospel. An unreached people group is a group with little to no access to the gospel, and with a population of less than 2 percent evangelical believers. Over 2.8 billion people fit this category. The majority of unreached people groups (85 percent) live in the 10/40 Window. The 10/40 Window is between latitudes 10 and 40 degrees north, from West Africa to East Asia.

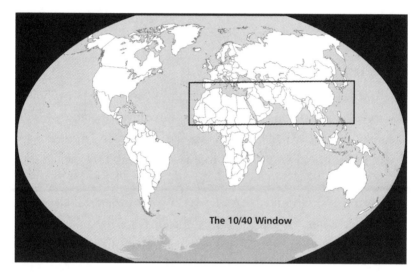

The 10/40 Window

All the people living in the 10/40 Window live within the stronghold of a major world religion other than Christianity. Most of the people you meet from the 10/40 Window will be from one of five cultural/religious blocs, which can be remembered by using the acronym THUMB: T for *Tribes*, H for *Hindu*, U (turn it on its side for a C) for *Chinese*, M for *Muslim*, and B for *Buddhist*.[4]

THE WORLD AS GOD SEES IT

Tribes: Two hundred-ninety million people are tribal, or animistic.[5] They believe spirits control the physical world.[6]

Tribal people believe in both good and bad spirits. Through worship, sacrifice, and rituals, one can manipulate the spirit world to gain favor or curse another. Most tribal groups have a spiritual witch doctor who is the mediator for the spirit world. They believe spirits can bestow themselves or their power into anything, but typically choose inanimate objects such as trees, rocks, and fire.

I can remember my first experience in the tribal world. Sitting by the fire, my friend said, "Do not touch anything while close to the villages: rocks, leaves, sticks, anything." I wondered why he was so adamant. He said one team member, while walking along the river the year before, picked up a rock and skipped it across the water. After watching it skip, he turned around to see a group of irritated tribesmen. He suddenly realized he had just thrown their deity into the water!

Tribal people are scattered in places like Papua New Guinea and parts of Africa and South America. Not only is the tribal world physically challenging to get to, their lifestyle is extremely difficult for outsiders to connect to. Of the world's nearly seven thousand languages, 71 percent of those are spoken by the tribal world.[7] Over eight hundred languages exist in Papua New Guinea alone, and a complete Bible exists for less than fifty of those. Tribal communities need people to come live with them, learn their language, and translate the Bible. The question I am challenged with is, "How would my life look without a Bible?" I wouldn't know about Jesus, the gospel, or the church. Yet this is the reality for most who live in the tribal world.

Hindu: Hinduism is the world's oldest religion. It began around 1500 BC. Hindus have been known to list 330 million different deities to worship.[8] The major books of Hinduism are the *Vedas*, the *Upanishads*, the *Laws of Manu*, and the *Bhagavad Gita*. Today, 900 million people call themselves Hindu.[9] Most live in India. Understanding their gods provides a little clarity amid the confusion.[10] Here is one story among the many.

Shiva, one of the top gods, had a wife named Parvati and a son named Ganesh. Shiva traveled on a long journey. Upon returning home, a man was standing outside his home. Thinking he was an intruder, Shiva drew his sword and severed the man's head. Parvati, hearing the commotion, ran outside and realized what had happened. Shiva had cut off the head of their son! Parvati turned and walked away in despair. Shiva vowed to take the head of the next thing that walked by and place it on Ganesh to heal him. The next thing he saw was an elephant. Shiva took the elephant's head and placed it on the shoulders of his son. Today, millions of people worship the elephant-headed god Ganesh. Hinduism is as diverse as its deities, and for a Hindu, worshipping Jesus isn't that difficult. Solely worshipping Jesus is!

Jason Mandryk, author of the country-specific prayer guide *Operation World*, was asked, "What are the top five most unreached countries in the world?" Mandryk replied, "India, India, India, India, China." Sobering, isn't it? This unmet need demands action.

Chinese: Obviously, Chinese is not a religion, but 1.3 billion Chinese people deserve their own category. One out of every six people on earth is Chinese. There are more teenagers in China than people in America.[11] There are more than 118 cities in China with populations over one million. Contrast this with Canada and the US combined, where only twelve cities are over a million. With so many people, China has two distinct sides: the antireligious and the super-religious. In cities and institutions, many adhere to the self-powering ethics of communism. It's not uncommon for young urban Chinese to grow up thinking, "There is no god. Believe in yourself."

On the other hand, throughout history China has been known for adherence to Confucianism, Daoism, and Buddhism. It is said, "Every Chinese wears a Confucian cap, a Daoist robe, and Buddhist sandals."[12] When reaching out to the Chinese, learning about each of these historic religions is not just helpful, it's necessary. The problem is most of the Chinese do not understand the full influence religion has had on them culturally. When asked, most would say they do not follow a religion. Dig a little deeper and you will see the historical religions have so permeated and affected them that the Chinese are almost unknowingly "Confucians at work, Daoists at leisure, and Buddhists at death."[13] More recently, in some locations Chinese believers have been allowed to gather weekly in public places to worship. Though there are between 50 and 100 million Christians in the country, this is a small percent of the total population.[14] For China, the harvest is still great and the laborers remain few.

Muslim: A follower of Islam is called a Muslim. Muslims believe the angel Gabriel gave a revelation from heaven to the prophet Muhammad ibn Abdullah in AD 610. Every devout Muslim practices the Five Pillars: prayer five times a day, fasting during the month of Ramadan, pilgrimage to Mecca, giving 2.5 percent of their income, and the declaration of belief "There is no god but God, and Muhammad is his prophet." The overall goal of Islam is submission to Allah, the Arabic word for God.

While in North Africa, I visited one of the world's oldest Islamic schools and saw some of the most notable mosques in the Islamic world. While there, I dialogued with a few men about Jesus. In one conversation a man said, "I know you believe that Jesus is God, but I will never believe He is anything more than a man." I remember thinking how daunting is the task of not only reaching these Muslims, but millions with the gospel who hold this paradigm. Unfortunately, most Muslims will never meet a Christian, never set eyes on a Bible, and never have someone walk them through the true life, death, and resurrection of Jesus. Multiple times each day, Muslims pray, "Show us the straight path." For most the answer never comes.

Buddhist: Today there are over 650 million Buddhists. I used to think Buddhism was the practice of rubbing a statue for good luck. I couldn't have been further from the truth. Siddhartha Gautama, the founder of the religion, was actually a Hindu man. To find the source of suffering in the world, Gautama left his family and studied under the top Hindu gurus for six years. Dissatisfied by these teachings, he sat under a tree in northern India and began to fast and meditate. Forty-nine days later, he awakened to the Middle Path: not living in extreme poverty or riches but taking the middle road. In Buddhism, the center point is the liberation of suffering. Gautama concluded that if people rid themselves of desire, they will then rid themselves of suffering. He became an enlightened one, a Buddha. Following this Middle Path, one will enter enlightenment, the final state of bliss, empty of all suffering. Within Buddhism, there are numerous practices, beliefs, books, and sects, but all aim to escape the suffering caused by rebirth. Concept-loaded Christian terms like "everlasting life" tend to be an obstacle Buddhists would refuse outright. Why would anyone want to live the life of suffering eternally? The gospel is simple, but the messenger can be confusing.

IS THERE HOPE?

Growing up, I was never enthusiastic about the outdoors. I remember my first camping trip. My initial response was "Why?" My family drove five hours to a state park filled with hills, trees, streams, and lakes. As soon as we set up the tent, my brother and I ran off into the woods. After what seemed like a few hours of exploring, I noticed the sun setting over the hills. We decided it was time to head back, but then we stopped. Which way to the campsite? My older, wiser eight-year-old brother was lost, and I was terrified. After some of the most grueling minutes of my life, my brother ran up the closest hill. Lagging behind I asked, "What are you looking for?" He said he remembered there was a water tower next to our campsite. If he could find the tower, he could find our parents. In the distance he saw it. With all our effort, we kept the water tower in our sights. It was our North Star. Just as the sun set, we walked into our campsite. That was the first time I ever got lost. And that is why I still don't go camping!

It's easy to get lost in the Christian life. We must have a water tower. A North Star. It gives us hope. It redirects our journey. Some of the most incredible sailors in history could navigate the oceans simply by using the stars. I still have trouble finding the Big Dipper. Luckily God has given a clear North Star in Revelation, showing us every nation, tribe, people, and language will worship Him (see Revelation 7:9).[15] Yet there are billions of people without the gospel. Sadly, less than 2.5 percent of foreign missionaries are working among unreached people.[16] Of all the money US Christians designate for "Christian causes," only 5.7 percent goes toward missions. And only six cents out of every one hundred dollars is allocated to the unreached![17] While there is vast need for funding, the greater need is for volunteers who will take the gospel to the unreached.

Though many Christians may never become long-term missionaries, the reality is God has commissioned each of us to live a missional life. Whether you live in Idaho or

Ireland, you have a part to play. For some it may be relocating geographically. For others it may be reallocating financially. I know a businessman in Texas who uses his bonus money every year to fund mobilizers recruiting missionaries. I know a girl in Iowa who befriended her Sudanese neighbors and through their friendship started reading the Bible with them. I know a family in Montana who invite Asian students into their home for a meal every few weeks. I know a college student from Oregon who started a weekly prayer group for unreached peoples. I know a small business owner in Tennessee who capped his salary and donates all of his extra income to missions. We all must play a part. We all must engage.

WHERE'S ILLYRICUM?

Paul's passion was to push the gospel to places it wasn't. He says from Jerusalem to Illyricum, "I have fully proclaimed the gospel of Christ" (Romans 15:19). Paul declared that from the city of Jerusalem all the way to the city of Illyricum he had successfully given access to the gospel to people within that region. What a statement! The distance between Jerusalem and Illyricum is roughly 1,400 miles. Was Paul saying he led all these people to Christ? No. That he shared the gospel with all of them? No. Rather, Paul established a foothold for the gospel in influential areas. His goal was to see the gospel available. The key word is *access*. If they have access, they have a chance to hear and respond. He followed up with, "And thus I aspired to preach the gospel, not where Christ was already named, so that I would not build on *another man's foundation*; but as it is written, 'They who had no news of Him shall see, and they who have not heard shall understand'" (Romans 15:20-21, NASB).

Paul wanted to see all peoples engaged by the gospel. He realized not everyone would come to the knowledge of truth, but his driving passion was to see Christ proclaimed and worshipped. John Piper, in his book *Let the Nations Be Glad*, reminds us to keep the unreached as priority: "God may have in mind that the aim of the rescue operation should be to gather saved sinners from every people in the world ... even if some of the successful rescuers must leave a fruitful *reached people* ... in order to labor among an (possibly less fruitful) *unreached people*."[18] God's plan includes all peoples! He desires to finish the task. This is the heartbeat of the church and should be the heartbeat of every believer.

On October 31, 2011, the United Nations honored Danica Camacho in Manila, Philippines, as a symbol that the world's population had reached seven billion. There are more people on earth today than ever in history. If we hold fast, our generation can impact more people than ever before. Our motivation to get involved and live strategically has never been greater! God's ultimate plan can be fulfilled in this generation. The question is, "Are you on board?"

ENDNOTES

1. Mark Woods, "Emmons on Target for Gold," *Juneau Empire*, August 22, 2004, http://www.juneauempire.com/.

2. Ralph Winter and Steven C. Hawthorne, *Perspectives on the World Christian Movement* (Pasadena, CA: William Carey Library, 1999), 535.

3. "Global Peoples Summary," Joshua Project, accessed March 29, 2013, http://joshuaproject.net/.

4. Bob Sjogren, *Unveiled At Last: Discover God's Hidden Message from Genesis to Revelation* (Seattle, WA: YWAM Publishing, 1992), 138.

5. Nearly 3 percent of the world's population according to David Barrett, *World Christian Encyclopedia: A Comparative Study of Churches and*

Religions in the Modern World, AD 1900-2000 (Nairobi: Oxford University Press, 1982), 582.

6. Dean Halverson, ed., *The Compact Guide to World Religions* (Minneapolis, MN: Bethany, 1996), 37.

7. David Sitton, *To Every Tribe with Jesus: Understanding and Reaching Tribal Peoples for Christ* (Sand Springs, OK: Grace and Truth Books, 2005), 4.

8. L. J. Baillas, *World Religions: A Story Approach* (Mystic, CT: Twenty-Third Publications, 1991), 158.

9. Stephen Prothero, *God Is Not One* (New York: HarperOne, 2011), 133.

10. Prothero, *God Is Not One*, 131.

11. Paul Borthwick, *Western Christians in Global Mission: What's the Role of the North American Church?* (Downers Grove, IL: IVP Books, 2012), 24.

12. J. J. Clarke, *The Tao of the West: Western Transformations of Taoist Thought* (London: Routledge, 2000), 22.

13. Prothero, *God Is Not One*, 103.

14. According to Mark Knoll in *The New Shape of World Christianity*, it is possible that more people attend church weekly in China than all of Europe combined. China now has one of the largest Bible-printing facilities in the world. The Chinese are becoming the new missionary force for reaching the nations, with nearly two dozen mission agencies and training facilities.

15. I am grateful for Claude Hickman for sharing this analogy with me. I was first introduced to this in his book *Live Life on Purpose* (Enumclaw, WA: WinePress, 2011).

16. David Barrett, Todd Johnson, Christopher Guidry, and Peter Crossing, *World Christian Trends, AD 30–AD 2200: Interpreting the Annual Christian Megacensus* (Pasadena, CA: William Carey Library, 2001), 40.

17. Barrett et al., *World Christian Trends*, 40.

18. John Piper, *Let the Nations Be Glad! The Supremacy of God in Missions* (Grand Rapids, MI: Baker, 2003), 168–169.

Chapter Four

Foxes Have Holes

Materialism

He will be known as one of the greatest quarterbacks of all time. In 2000, twenty-three-year-old Tom Brady was picked late in the draft by the New England Patriots. A year later, he got the starting position. After three games Brady hit his stride. There was no stopping him. By the time Brady was twenty-eight, he had won three Super Bowls. He was at the top of his game, reaching accomplishments most could only dream of. At the height of his success, Brady said, "I'm making more money now than I ever thought I could playing football." Yet Brady wasn't fulfilled. He stated, "Why do I have three Super Bowl rings and still think there is something greater out there for me? I mean … it's got to be more than this."[1]

Tom Brady had the life most long for. He was the epitome of the American Dream. He had everything, only to still be lacking. So why do we all strive for it? The American Dream is one of the toughest obstacles we face in the pursuit of Christ. We live in a culture more saturated with a vision of retirement than eternity. For many the American Dream is the pursuit of a well-paying job, a good-looking spouse, a house in the suburbs, three kids, two dogs, and nice cars. Though the American

Dream may individually play out differently, the pursuit is the same: our satisfactions and pleasures being found in something other than Christ.

As Westerners we feel if we can earn it, we deserve it. As followers of Christ we are called to live life counterculturally and not focus on the American Dream. Our goal as believers is to leverage our lives, ambitions, blessings, earnings, and finances so the gospel may advance.

The lure of the American Dream is an iceberg. An iceberg is magnificent. It beckons our attention with its beauty. The trouble is icebergs can be hard to see. They are, after all, mostly underwater! We don't realize they're there till it's too late. The risk of material gain isn't worth sinking our ship. Our intention must be to stay on course by avoiding materialism for the sake of finishing the mission.

The Bible is laced with verses about living for eternity. Paul alerted Timothy about the pleasures of the world:

> But godliness with contentment is great gain, for we brought nothing into the world, and we cannot take anything out of the world.... But those who desire to be rich fall into temptation, into a snare, into many senseless and harmful desires that plunge people into ruin and destruction. (1 Timothy 6:6,9, ESV)

He continued warning us about money:

> For the love of money is a root of all kinds of evils. It is through this craving that some have wandered away from the faith and pierced themselves with many pangs. But as for you, O man of God, flee these things. (vv. 10-11, ESV)

Paul took it a step further and told Timothy how to guard himself: "Pursue righteousness.... Take hold of the eternal life to which you were called" (vv. 11-12). We are to guard ourselves from the pitfall of greed by pursuing righteousness and a proper view of eternity. When we have an inaccurate view of this life, we derive a false sense of hope.

Money can destroy us. But is money evil? God warns that money can bring us to destruction, but it's not the money that ruins. It is the *love of money* that is the root of all kinds of evil. Money may corrupt us if we love it, or it can lead to eternal glory if we invest it eternally (see vv. 17-20). Avoid the iceberg. Hold fast to the future reward.

We measure the value of something by what we are willing to give for it. Consider the rich young ruler and his conversation with Christ:

> And a ruler asked him, "Good Teacher, what must I do
> to inherit eternal life?" And Jesus said to him, "Why do
> you call me good? No one is good except God alone.
> You know the commandments: 'Do not commit adultery,
> Do not murder, Do not steal, Do not bear false witness,
> Honor your father and mother.'"

The rich young ruler replied,

> "All these I have kept from my youth." When Jesus
> heard this, he said to him, "One thing you still lack. Sell
> all that you have and distribute to the poor, and you will
> have treasure in heaven; and come, follow me."
> (Luke 18:18-22, ESV)

Jesus was not saying you must be poor to enter the kingdom of God. Jesus wasn't after the money. His point was the ruler's identity and security were in his wealth. Money is not the ultimate pursuit; the kingdom is. At times riches stand in the way. This is why Jesus warned, "It is easier for a camel to go through the eye of a needle than for a rich person to enter the kingdom of God" (Luke 18:25, esv). We must love Christ more than riches. Jesus said, "The kingdom of heaven is like treasure hidden in a field, which a man found and covered up. Then in his joy he goes and sells all that he has and buys that field" (Matthew 13:44, esv). If the kingdom of heaven is of such great value, then the loss of all things to get it, no matter how painful, is not a tragedy.[2]

The Bible warns us that abandoning the mission causes us to lose sight of Christ. Take Demas, for example. He was a fellow worker of Paul in spreading the gospel. Paul mentioned him three times in his letters, the first two times in a respectable way (see Colossians 4:14; Philemon 1:24), but the third time Paul wrote, "For Demas, in love with this present world, has deserted me and gone to Thessalonica" (2 Timothy 4:10, esv). He not only stopped laboring with Paul, he deserted him for the pleasures of the world. Paul took the time to write other believers about this deserter and the trap of money. For most, like Demas, the temptation is subtle. Materialism is rarely a blatant excuse. I've never had anyone say to me, "I would love to be enlisted in God's mission, but I'm materialistic and am completely fixed on my personal satisfaction." Most people never acknowledge being controlled by the pursuit of ease. Materialism is a silent excuse.

The tough part is not saying good-bye to the nice car, but saying yes to living in a village with no running water, no electricity, no relatives, and no medical aid. Or living in a low-income area filled with drugs or sex offenders. That's a very tough "yes." Putting your wife, kids, and self in the "no insurance policy" part of the world isn't what most consider wise. We like our multifunctioning electronics and our trendy clothes, but more importantly, we like living comfortably. We value the security of knowing we and our loved ones will be safe. Material comforts give us that false sense of security. Materialism, for all of us, lurks around each corner. Hold fast.

Consider the response of Christ when an eager and passionate person asked to follow Him: "As they were going along the road, someone said to him, 'I will follow you wherever you go.' And Jesus said to him, 'Foxes have holes, and birds of the air have nests, but the Son of Man has nowhere to lay his head'" (Luke 9:57-58, ESV). Most would not be expecting this response after offering their life in service to God. I would have expected Jesus to respond quite the opposite. I would have thought His response would be, "Let's go! I've been looking for someone with faith like yours." But Jesus knows our hearts. He cuts through the flattery. Jesus simply says those who want the securities of this world don't trust in the provisions of God.

Hudson Taylor, one of the most notable missionaries to China, once said, "God's work done in God's ways will never lack God's supplies."[3] This echoes Christ's words "The Son of Man has nowhere to lay his head," meaning, "I don't have a home and a bed to sleep in, because this is not My home." We who are Christ's disciples should not expect our lives to be any less missional than His.

MEDICAL SCHOOL OR MISSIONS

Growing up, my best friend was Will. We played T-ball together, stayed the night at each other's house, even liked the same girls. We were *best* friends. Going into college Will had one thing on his mind: medical school. His major was biochemistry, and his minor was Spanish. With his GPA and talent, he was med school-bound. His vision for the future was well thought out. He wanted to establish an orthopedic surgery practice on the slopes of Vail, Colorado. It seemed perfect.

While in college he started going to a Bible study where they would pray for the world. He then met international students. Slowly Will's heart started shifting. Before graduating he was faced with a decision: medical school or Asia. Upon graduating, Will waved good-bye to his MD and the slopes of Vail and said hello to Asia. I asked Will if he ever regrets the decision he made, giving up his dream for God's. He replied, "I've never made a sacrifice. The dream that I had for myself pales in comparison to what God has in store for me." Will faced a tough decision—his glory or God's. Ironically, I even argued with him, "Will, you're crazy. Your dream isn't even that selfish! Minus the location, you just want to help others and serve your community. Think of all the good you can do with a medical degree!" For Will, it wasn't about helping his community, or even his occupation. It was about aligning his life with God's and taking the gospel where it wasn't.

Now meet Jonathan. Jonathan faced a situation similar to Will's. Wanting to go to the harder places, he realized a medical degree provided the perfect platform. So postgraduation, Jonathan decided to go back to college, get a degree in biology, and go to medical school. This decision will postpone his living overseas for at least eight years, but for Jonathan it will make the most impact. Jonathan will be a doctor who will live, work, and raise his kids in places like North Africa. Medical school is not wrong if the reasons are right.

We all have decisions that can help or hurt our relationship with Christ. Test yourself. Whose dreams are you following? In the end, are you more worried about God's glory or your own? Will your vision, if it comes to fruition, help the gospel reach the world?

A SEEMINGLY WASTED LIFE

William Borden was born in 1887 to wealthy parents who raised him in the Christian faith. Upon graduation from high school, William was fortunate enough to take a sailing trip around the world. On this trip he went to Africa, Arabia, and Asia. He saw poverty and fortune, sickness and health, and religions of all kinds. His experience showed him the only answer for all people was the cross of Christ. He flipped to the back of his Bible and wrote the phrase "No Reserves." After this trip William returned home to attend Yale University. After graduation he was to inherit the family business, Borden Milk Products. It was a life most could only dream of. But William couldn't get past his experience abroad. Despite the riches awaiting him, he decided to invest his life toward making a difference. He started praying for those who had never heard the gospel and for students on his campus. He lived in such a way that no one would know he was a millionaire's son. He lived humbly and challenged others to give their lives for the only thing that lasts—Christ. He once wrote in his journal, "Say 'no' to self and 'yes' to Jesus every time."[4] One classmate wrote of William Borden,

> He came to college far ahead, spiritually, of any of us. He
> had already given his heart in full surrender to Christ....
> We who were his classmates learned to lean on him
> and find in him a strength that was solid as a rock, just
> because of this settled purpose and consecration.[5]

William's prayer time slowly expanded during his freshman year to include his roommate, then another friend, and then others. By the end of the year the prayer group included 150 students. This prayer group continued through his senior year, and by his last semester, 1,000 of Yale's 1,300 students were meeting weekly for prayer and Bible study. He also founded Yale Hope Mission, which reached beyond the walls of Yale to the poor, the homeless, and the disabled. Borden rescued as many as he could: drunks, widows, and orphans. His friend wrote that Borden "might often be found in the lower parts of the city at night, on the street, in a cheap lodging house or some restaurant to which he had taken a poor hungry fellow to feed him, seeking to lead men to Christ."[6]

William Borden constantly entreated his friends and classmates to consider going overseas as missionaries. He focused on taking the gospel to the Muslims of China, and he informed his parents he would not be taking over the family business. Following an intense argument with his father, Borden signed over his inheritance. After his decision, he opened his Bible again and wrote "No Retreats." Borden traveled the US for three months recruiting for missions. He packed his possessions, boarded a boat, and headed east. En route to China, he stopped in Egypt to learn Arabic. His third month in Egypt, Borden contracted spinal meningitis. Within a month, William Borden was dead. He was twenty-five. His possessions were gathered and shipped to his family. His mother found his Bible. Thumbing through it, she found written on the back page "No Reserves," "No Retreats," and, written only days before his death, "No Regrets."[7]

Borden's life and death circled the world, from Egypt to China to America. He inspired thousands to live for the gospel. Many people thought he wasted his life. His tombstone in

Egypt reads otherwise: "Apart from faith in Christ, there is no explanation for such a life. Mark 16:15." With the American Dream and the rewards of the world at his fingertips, William Borden had everything he could ever dream of, yet it wasn't fulfilling. He wanted to live a life worthy of eternity. He knew heaven would be filled with praises from every nation, tribe, people, and language. William Borden held fast to the mission.

Steer clear of the superficial beauty of the American Dream and the allure of stuff. In the end it is shallow and deceptive. Set your sights on the reward of Christ and hold fast.

ENDNOTES

1. Tom Brady, interview by Steve Kroft, *60 Minutes*, CBS, June 2005.
2. This quote was adapted from Matt Chandler's sermon "Buying the Field," Village Church, June 23, 2007.
3. Howard Taylor, *Hudson Taylor and the China Inland Mission* (London: Morgan and Scott Ltd., 1920), 42.
4. Mrs. Howard Taylor, *Borden of Yale* (Philadelphia, China Inland Mission, 1946), 122.
5. Mrs. Howard Taylor, *Borden of Yale*, 98.
6. Mrs. Howard Taylor, *Borden of Yale*, 148.
7. Howard Culbertson "No Reserves, No Retreats, No Regrets." For more original content like this, visit: http://home.snu.edu/~hculbert.

Chapter Five

A Suitable Helper
Relationships

"You will marry *someone* that you date."[1] I had to repeat it twice when I heard it. Simple, but profound. It is a statement we should hear and say often. Relationships are a massive hindrance to missional living. Yet, most never consider a relationship as an obstacle to obedience. Many people are derailed from the mission because they fall in love with the wrong person. Molly's view of dating was a little different. She started dating Jim, a non-Christian. Molly was hopeful that he would change his mind. Their relationship progressed. Jim proposed and Molly couldn't resist. Jim never became a Christian and Molly's passions slowly changed.

Obedience to God must be a higher priority than getting married. If the person you desire to date is not obeying God, they are not a candidate for dating. In dating, world vision must be a nonnegotiable or you are setting yourself up for a rough relationship. Easier said than done, I agree.

It's easy to say, "No vision, no date" when you are surrounded by a dozen like-minded, global-Christian, disciple-making people. It seems completely different when you're thirty-five and you've only been on three dates in ten years. You cry out, "Lord, where are the godly singles?" You start thinking deeply on the phrase "single life" and realize it may mean "single *for* life." However, there is something worse than being single for the rest of your life—marrying the wrong person!

In college I was eager to join the rowing team. My enthusiasm quickly faded when I found out practice was at five a.m. What college student wakes up that early? There were three types of rowing teams: two-, four-, and eight-person teams. In some sports, an individual can carry the whole team. In rowing, the team works together as a single unit. The most important number in rowing is the rows per minute. The two-person teams are the most intense. With only two spots on each boat, the coach is able to handpick the best individuals for the team. Marriage is a two-person rowing team. Dating the wrong type of person is like willfully choosing a bad teammate. Who does this? We need a teammate who will help us finish well. Hold fast for a missional Christian.

Hudson Taylor was a pioneer missionary to inland China. When he made up his mind about going overseas, he told his girlfriend. Her response was, "Must you go to China? How much nicer it would be to stay and serve the Lord at home."[2] She made it plain she would not go to China. She was probably known at the time as Hudson Taylor's newest ex-girlfriend.

Roberta Winter, cofounder of the US Center for World Mission and mother of four daughters, wrote, "Let your relationship bring honor to God in its purity and its concern for the world. Don't get anxious. Believe that God is in the matchmaking business (isn't He), and that He knows what He is about. In the meantime, relax and glorify Him."[3]

What does the Bible explicitly say about dating? Actually, nothing. Though some people long to find the random verse and make it apply: "You will go out with joy" (Isaiah 55:12, NASB). Whether or not they know a girl named Joy makes no difference to them.

What does the Bible say about marriage and relationships? Actually, a lot. "That is why a man leaves his father and mother and is united to his wife, and they become one flesh" (Genesis 2:24). From the very beginning God's goal was for man and woman to be united as one. Hebrews states, "Marriage should be honored by all" (Hebrews 13:4), meaning the marriage commitment should not be treated as routine. In God's eyes marriage is precious. Marriage is the living symbol of the gospel. Ephesians says, "Husbands, love your wives, just as Christ loved the church and gave himself up for her" (Ephesians 5:25). The sanctity and meaning of marriage are significant. So, what does this mean for dating?

Some people date because they are lonely or bored, but we should always date with a view of marriage in mind. Dating is one of the blessings of singleness. Dating should be fun. You have the privilege to get to know someone before saying "I do." It is a chance to spend time with someone you wouldn't otherwise have the opportunity to get to know. But before you begin looking *for* the right type of person, you need to *be* the right type of person. To do this, author Ken Graves says you must have three things in order: Master, mission, mate.[4]

First and foremost, you need to decide who your *Master* is. Who are you submitting to? Jesus needs to be Lord of your life. If there's some pursuit or interest that is not subjugated under His rule we will have problems.

Once we know whom we are following, we need to know our *mission*. Jesus tells His followers to "make disciples of all nations" (Matthew 28:19). God is not so worried about what profession you choose or where you live. He is far more interested in you dedicating your talents, time, and resources to fulfill the Great Commission. Marriage is God's idea! God said, "It is not good for the man to be alone. I will make a helper suitable for him" (Genesis 2:18). Adam wasn't out beating the bushes, but instead was doing what God had told him to do: naming the animals (v. 19). All the animals were brought to him, yet none was a "suitable helper" for Adam (v. 20). So God designed Eve, his *mate*, and "brought her" to him (v. 22). Adam was being obedient to God's commands, and God brought Adam and Eve together. When we are submitted to the Master and pursuing His mission, He provides what we need most.

MARRIAGE AND THE MISSION

"Who you marry will make you or break you."[5] What does a person do if they are married to someone with little or no world vision? This is a very difficult question. Here is a message we recently received:

> I just wanted to let you know I came across your website today. At 18, I spent a summer in student missions and knew at the end of that summer that God wanted me in missions work—but then I met "a guy" and basically sold God out just to get married. I am now 41 and have regretted that decision in so many ways. Please keep telling young people that the day to minister for Christ is TODAY—not tomorrow or next semester or next year. And tell them to never, ever, ever let any person or any thing deter you from the mission that God has placed in your heart. I am speaking from experience.

This woman is in a tough spot. No one thinks they will end up here. How are we to respond? At times the biggest obstacle to believers is never having heard God's passion for the world. Knowledge precedes passion. "God cannot lead us... on the basis of facts we do not know."[6] Help your spouse. Pray for God to burden their heart for the world. Most importantly, make sure their most important relationship is their relationship with Christ. If they are passionately seeking Him, their heart will change. They might not go to the mission field, but they will play a part. If you are married to a nonbeliever, pray for them. Serve them. Love them. Never get angry with them. Scolding doesn't mobilize. Until they become a follower of Christ, they will never desire to obey God.

DISQUALIFIED

Proverbs warns, "Guard your heart above all else" (Proverbs 4:23, NLT). Guard your own heart, but also the heart of the one you date. I pursued a girl my senior year of college. After a few weeks, I asked her if I could hold her hand. She said yes. I almost fainted. That question opened up a conversation about physical and emotional boundaries. In the midst of the conversation, she said, "I prayed about whether or not I should hold your hand this soon. I really wrestled with this. I've been asking the Lord if holding your hand would lead us closer to Christ." Wow! I never prayed about holding a girl's hand. Never had I thought about this simple thing being a matter of physical or spiritual purity. The Bible says, "There must not be even a hint of sexual immorality" (Ephesians 5:3). Not even a hint. None. She was obedient to that.

Have an intentional conversation with the one you are dating regarding the boundaries of your relationship. Never do something you haven't talked about previously. If you haven't talked about kissing, don't kiss. If you haven't talked about holding hands, don't hold hands. If you do, you risk not guarding your heart. If you are prone to fall into temptation, you should plan some distractions, add some company, avoid temptations, or only go on public dates.

We all struggle with sexual sins. Marriage will not solve your struggles with impurity. The truth is if you don't solve your sexual purity issues before you marry, you will carry them into marriage. For many, sexual sin will sideline them from the mission of God. Marriage is not the solution to sexual impurity. Jesus is. No matter your sins, God redeems and can use us for His glory. "In the same way, count yourselves dead to sin but alive to God in Christ Jesus.... For sin shall no longer be your master, because you are not under the law, but under grace" (Romans 6:11, 14). End sin's reign in your body by keeping your affections on Christ.

> Therefore, since we are surrounded by such a great cloud
> of witnesses, let us throw off everything that hinders
> and the sin that so easily entangles. And let us run with
> perseverance the race marked out for us, fixing our eyes on
> Jesus, the pioneer and perfecter of faith. (Hebrews 12:1-2)

By fixing our eyes on Christ, we lay aside the weight and sin that can overcome us. Take the precautions and actions necessary to avoid temptation. Christ reminds us, "Anyone who looks at a woman lustfully has already committed adultery with her in his heart" (Matthew 5:28). Prevent sin before it happens. If you fail, seek accountability and repent from your sins.

WOMEN AND MINISTRY: THOUGHTS FROM SARAH
Throughout history, one word describes women's involvement in missions: obedience. Women have been the driving force in missions. Two-thirds of the mission force has been, and currently is, female.[7] Missions-mobilizer Sarah Allen has sat down with hundreds of women to discuss their involvement in missions. She has given me her insight about women in ministry through the rest of this chapter:

The fact that so many women are getting involved in ministry is amazing. There have been quite a few questions when it comes to women in ministry. I've identified consistent themes, which can be boiled down to the Three C's: companionship, culture, and community.

The most obvious issue is *companionship*. When I signed up for ministry, I feared I was signing up for singleness. I committed to living out of a suitcase, traveling around the country, out of sight and out of mind for any godly single men that I knew. But I'm not the only one who thinks about this. Here's how the conversations go:

> Hey Sarah, I'm so ready to graduate. Right now I am really thinking about doing campus ministry or cross-cultural missions. Possibly for life! Another thing that has really been on my mind is how this will impact my love life. Within my group of girlfriends two are engaged, two are dating, and leaving two of us single. It makes my heart nervous that I don't even have a date. I have never even been in a serious relationship. I'm not exactly a boy-crazy type of girl, but this is definitely something that has been on my mind recently. Any thoughts on your end?

When it comes to the question of relationships, I understand. On one hand, I know that God works outside of our time and circumstances for His purposes. No matter where in the world we end up, if He wants us to be married, we will get married. God doesn't need our help to run into the man of our dreams. We need to trust Him.

However, I do warn against expectations. This could be our biggest cause of pain. God could drop a godly man in our lap at any moment, but we shouldn't be staring at the sky while waiting for it. Scripture and testimonies speak clearly about how God uses single women to minister in a way that married women cannot. If God wants you single, do not expect that to change. Do not look forward to the day it will change. Seek contentment in your singleness, and joy will come from devoting your time and energy to ministry.

> An unmarried woman or virgin is concerned about the
> Lord's affairs: Her aim is to be devoted to the Lord in
> both body and spirit. But a married woman is concerned
> about the affairs of this world—how she can please
> her husband. I am saying this for your own good, not
> to restrict you, but that you may live in a right way in
> undivided devotion to the Lord. (1 Corinthians 7:34-35)

A desire to be married is good. Desiring marriage as an answer to our discontentment is idolatry. A boyfriend, a husband, children, a comfortable home, a great wardrobe, a degree—nothing will truly satisfy us except for Christ. Like all areas of our life, God desires our obedience, but more than that He desires heart change. He wants us to *want* Him above all! I want to be married, and that's okay. But my desire is to first seek God's kingdom and His righteousness.

As you learn to be obedient to Christ and to make His name known, you will want someone who desires the same. It's better to be married to the right man for forty years than the wrong man for fifty. And it's better to wish you married than to wish you were single. I know godly women who have fallen off the map and out of ministry for the sake of a less-than-worthy boyfriend, fiancé, or husband. That breaks my heart.

Culture is another inhibiting factor of women in ministry.

There are countries around the world that make it especially difficult for American women to live what Westerners consider a normal life. Going to the market, the gym, the coffee shop, or even work can be stressful because everything must be done in groups of women or with your husband. Some cultures also value extreme modesty, which seems initially to be no problem. But what happens when we find ourselves in a country that is 120 degrees but requires covering from wrists to ankles?

Paul encourages Christians to do what needs to be done to reach people for Christ: "To the Jews I became like a Jew, to win the Jews" (1 Corinthians 9:20). This means to the Muslim, we must become like the Muslim in cultural ways. Paul says he submits himself to these cultural regulations for the greatest good: "I have become all things to all people so that by all possible means I might save some" (v. 22).

The third obstacle is *community*. Though many girls think finding Mr. Right is going to greatly help, the driving force behind life is our girlfriends. Everything is done in groups. Best friends, Bible studies, small groups, and life groups—we have our girls we talk to for the sake of keeping our sanity. Consider going to the more difficult areas. Community naturally shrinks. There may be only a small number of believers in the city; what then? Thankfully, with the blessing of technology we can connect to nearly anyone, anywhere in the world.

For me, I found myself in a different city every week. I quickly realized the need to find people for debriefing and encouragement. The writer of Hebrews said, "Let us consider how we may spur one another on toward love and good deeds, not giving up meeting together … but encouraging one another" (10:24-25). I recruited three women I could call at particular times throughout the week. Not only was it good for me, but it helped me refocus on ministry and grow in my relationship with Christ. For some it might mean seeking out people to call. For others, it might mean getting into a small group. Regardless, the call to community is unquestionable. These obstacles can easily inhibit us from effective ministry, but planning for how to work through them is prudent. God blesses us in different ways. Sometimes the gift is singleness. Sometimes it's marriage. It must be Christ who decides, not us!

Grace Wilder was a student at Mount Holyoke College in 1886. Being the daughter of a missionary, she knew the realities of the field and the cost of going. Grace prayed God would use her on her campus to ignite a fire in the lives of other women. She drafted a commitment card and required other women to sign it to be in her Bible study. It read, "We hold ourselves willing and desirous, to go wherever the Lord may call us, even if it be in the foreign lands." Throughout her college career, she had thirty girls sign the commitment. Grace stayed faithful to her commitment. At twenty-six, she and her widowed mother packed their bags and moved to India. Grace spent the rest of her life as an unmarried missionary. Her life serves as a Christ-like challenge for the women of God to this day.

ENDNOTES

1. [Steve Shadrach], *Brown Like Coffee: For Students Who Think Outside the Box* (Fayetteville, AR: self-published, 2007), 82.
2. Howard Taylor, *Hudson Taylor and the China Inland Mission* (London: Morgan and Scott Ltd., 1920), 110.
3. Roberta Winter, "Dating," The Traveling Team, accessed March 29, 2013, http://www.thetravelingteam.org/.
4. Ken Graves, *Master, Mission, Mate: A Guide for Christian Singles* (Orrington, ME: Calvary Chapel Bangor, 2006).

5. Steve Shadrach, Director of the Center for Mission Mobilization, shared this with me in one of our many conversations.

6. David Bryant, *In the Gap* (Ventura, CA: Regal, 1979), 55.

7. Ralph Winter and Steven Hawthorne, *Perspectives on the World Christian Movement* (Pasadena, CA: William Carey Library, 1999), 296.

Chapter Six

<u>   </u>

Your Mother Is Outside
Family

What do you do when God says go, but family says no? How do you reconcile obedience to your parents and obedience to the Lord? How difficult the words, "Whoever loves father or mother more than me is not worthy of me, and whoever loves son or daughter more than me is not worthy of me" (Matthew 10:37, ESV).

Just as the quest for a mate keeps many from obeying God, an unsupportive, unenthusiastic family may also stand between you and God's will. This is one of the toughest obstacles to overcome. There are countless stories of family members who manipulated loved ones using every emotional, physical, scriptural, and psychological strategy. Boundaries don't always exist when it comes to parents trying to keep their kids from missional living, especially if that entails moving overseas. One missionary said,

> Pretty much every week before leaving, my wife's mother
> used to send her a message trying to dissuade her from
> going to the mission field. Her mother told her she
> is taking away all her happiness by taking away her
> grandson. Her mom frequently tells her she cries herself
> to sleep every night. She also told her the number one

factor in her mom's unhappiness was our decision to
go to the mission field. This has been extremely hard
on my wife and on me.

The sad reality is this is only the beginning. Family
and friends may not consider what you do to even be a
job. They may assume this is another bad idea or another
whimsical choice in your young adult life. Parents may be
ashamed because their son or daughter must raise financial
support. They may ask you not to raise money from their
friends. Some even put obstacles in your way, not making
payments they may have committed to for college, or even
not allowing you to go on the family vacation. Ouch.
Nothing is off-limits. Sadly, throughout history Christian
parents have been an obstacle. Could you live in a foreign
country knowing your family disapproves? Todd Ahrend,
author of *In This Generation*, said, "The possibility that
Christian parents are the number one hindrance to world
evangelization is truer than we would like to admit."[1]

Jesus faced the same issue. He balanced being submissive
to his parents and engaging in ministry, yet Jesus valued the
kingdom of God more than family:

> And his mother and his brothers came, and standing
> outside they sent to him and called him. And a
> crowd was sitting around him, and they said to him,
> "Your mother and your brothers are outside, seeking
> you." And he answered them, "Who are my mother
> and my brothers?" And looking about at those who
> sat around him, he said, "Here are my mother and my
> brothers! For whoever does the will of God, he is my
> brother and sister and mother." (Mark 3:31-35, ESV)

Jesus loved His mother and brothers. His point was not that their relationship was not meaningful, but their relationship was not as valuable as the mission. Jesus came to the world to give His life. This took precedence.

Family isn't always negative. Family should be our anchor. Boat anchors are a necessity. Every ship has two types of anchors: temporary anchors and deadweight anchors. Temporary anchors are small. They can be dropped at any time to keep a ship from drifting, even in the most extreme weather. Deadweight anchors are gigantic blocks of cement that keep boats in the marina. Our family should be a temporary anchor, calming our ship in the storms of life. However, in trying to keep loved ones from the dangers of the ocean, some are never released from the dock. Too many families are deadweight anchors, never letting their ship out of the marina for the very purpose for which it was created.

TWO TYPES OF PARENTS

Parents who say no to their son or daughter living missionally fall into two categories, those who mean it and those who don't. The ones who mean it try to leverage everything in their power so their child will not leave. They leverage finances, vehicles, inheritances, or even holiday get-togethers. If you are still young and under their authority, I would advise talking with them and waiting until they are softened to the idea. In the meantime, pray for them. Keep them informed. Introduce them to key people who hold your values.

The other category of parents say no as an indicator to see if their child is serious about this decision or if it's just another phase. They may relate your desire to do ministry to poor decisions you've made in the past. The difference with this type of parent is they are being consistently informed and are open to what God is doing in your life. They see you taking responsible steps toward living missionally. Parents tend to grow more confident in their child's decision when they see them maturing. The majority of parents fall into this second category. To hold fast in difficulty of family, keep them informed.

Rebecca Hickman, who has counseled hundreds of women regarding missions, addresses obedience and submission to parents by saying,

> Culturally, there comes a time when you gradually move out from under your parents' authority and make decisions for yourself. For some it occurs when they graduate college and move into their own career. For others it comes with getting married. The timing is different for everyone, so you must discern for yourself where you are in relation to your parents…. Sometimes the greatest witness your parents can see is you fully obeying the call of God on your life.[2]

If your parents still don't concede and never consent to letting you go, you must obey the Lord first. If He leads you to go, cling to the promises of God. You are not alone.

Tonya was a sophomore in college. She wanted to go on a short-term trip for the summer, but her parents didn't think it would be safe. Her dad wasn't against missions; he just felt responsible for her safety. If she went on the trip, he couldn't protect her. To respect her parents, she decided not to go. She prayed for her parents for three years and had intentional conversations about going overseas. Tonya's dad attended a conference and heard a speaker talk about the world. The speaker said, "I've been working with college students for thirty years, and the number one reason they fail to get involved in God's heart for the nations is because of Christian parents." He was convicted. On the way home, he called Tonya and promised, "I will never stand in the way of what God is doing again."

Tonya moved to Southeast Asia. While in Asia, God was still working on her parents. When she returned home, Tonya's dad had some news. Mom and dad were moving to Asia! Her parents quit their jobs, boarded a plane, and took up residence in Asia. Oh, how faithless we can be when faced with our own obstacles. Tonya trusted the Lord, and He provided beyond what she could ever ask or imagine.

C. T. Studd was a household name in the late 1800s. He was one of the best cricketeers in England. While in college at Cambridge University, C. T. became a believer and heard about the spiritual needs in China. Studd decided to quit cricket and go to China. In the process, he recruited his teammates. They were known as the Cambridge Seven. The nation of England was stunned. Before Studd set sail, his father passed away. His brother, a faithful Christian, tried to persuade him not to go. Though C. T. believed God was leading him to China, he hesitated because of his widowed mother. C. T. prayed until God gave him a verse: "A man's enemies are the men of his own house" (Micah 7:6, ESV). After that he never looked back.[3] Charles Thomas Studd went to China as a missionary. He spent ten years in China, six years in India, and eighteen years in Africa.

If parents are an obstacle for you, here are seven ideas Rebecca Hickman suggests we remember as we ask God to change their hearts:

1. Ask them to pray with you for a few months about your plans.
2. Ask them why they feel as they do. Seriously consider their reasons. Since they raised you and know your character better than anyone else, they may see major problems with your plans that you hadn't realized.
3. Seek counsel from an older Christian who knows your family. They may have some insight about how to approach your parents.
4. Introduce them to a staff member of the agency you would choose, and let them ask questions.
5. Express your gratitude for the things they have provided for you in the past.
6. Show appreciation for the sacrifices they will be making when you go.
7. Let your family know that you haven't just dismissed their objections.[4]

Jeff, a sophomore at Arizona State University, knew he wanted to go overseas. He took a semester off from college and spent six months in Tanzania. When he returned, he went back to school but wanted to be a full-time missionary. His parents thought it was just a phase and emphatically said no. Jeff reasoned with them and prayed for them for weeks. Still no. While in college, he decided to go on another short-term trip, and this time his parents financially cut him off. Jeff was now responsible for paying for loans his parents had committed to pay. After a year of praying for his family, their hearts changed. They realized how hard he was working and heard stories of how God was using him. After many conversations, his relationship with his parents turned around. The tension between balancing relationships while we seek to obey God tends to push us to our knees.

Family was an obstacle for me. As I was growing up, my parents exemplified faithful believers. After my first year in college, I wanted to go on a summer discipleship project. They agreed wholeheartedly. The next summer, God led me to India. My parents said no problem. Before departing for India, my parents and I had a difficult discussion. This would be my last trip while in college. I had to commit all breaks and summers to family and work. They were not mad at me or against the mission of God. My parents objected because they loved me and didn't see me enough. Family isn't always an unholy obstacle. Deep down they want to be around you ... a lot.

In 1810, Adoniram Judson was courting his girlfriend, Ann. He was committed to God, Ann, and sailing to India. The greatest obstacle to them going overseas was her father. Judson desired to get his consent to marriage. Would her father give the blessing? Judson sent a letter to him:

> I have now to ask, whether you can consent to part
> with your daughter early next Spring to see her
> no more in this world; whether you can consent
> to her departure, and her subscription to the
> hardships and sufferings of missionary life; whether
> you can consent to her exposure to the dangers of
> the ocean; to the fatal influence of the southern
> climate of India; to every kind of want and distress;
> to degradation, insult, persecution, and perhaps a
> violent death. Can you consent to all this, for the
> sake of him who left his heavenly home, and died for

her and for you; for the sake of perishing, immortal
souls; for the sake of Zion, and the glory of God?

Judson continued the appeal,

Can you consent to all this, in hope of soon meeting
your daughter in the world of glory, with the crown
of righteousness, brightened with the acclamations
of praise which shall redound to her Saviour from
heathens saved, through her means, from eternal
woe and despair?[5]

Bold words to a father. Judson showed Ann's father he
was the only thing standing between them and the gospel
going to Asia. The couple was married on February 5, 1812,
and within a week of their wedding they set sail for India.

Some things Jesus said are difficult to understand. The
crowds were often confused, saying, "This is a hard teaching.
Who can accept it?" (John 6:60). When speaking about
family, Jesus stated, "If anyone comes to me and does not
hate his own father and mother and wife and children and
brothers and sisters, yes, and even his own life, he cannot
be my disciple" (Luke 14:26, ESV). Do you actually have to
hate your family to follow Jesus? Of course not. He means
there will be things you do in your pursuit of obedience
to God that makes it look like you hate your family. Your
priority, love, and devotion are now to the kingdom of God.
To the world this can look like hate. Missing your brother's
wedding so you can minister in the Middle East. Missing
holidays with family so you can serve at the homeless
shelter. Missing funerals, births, and birthdays for the

sake of the gospel reaching the nations. This is the cost of discipleship. This is the cost of obedience.

James was a junior in college when he took a year off to go to India. At the beginning, his parents were hesitant, but they agreed to let him go. While in India, James and a friend were riding a scooter back to their apartment when a car crossed lanes and hit them head-on. His friend died instantly, and James sustained severe injuries. The next three weeks James's life teetered on the edge of death. God miraculously healed him, bringing him back to health. He returned to America to finish rehab. After four months James shocked everyone. He wanted to go back to India. For him the decision was simple, but not for his parents. James's parents were afraid to let him go. They had nearly lost him once. Now they were faced with him leaving again. What would happen? Would he make it back this time? Questions like these overwhelmed them. A few weeks before leaving, James awoke to his mother quietly crying. James realized this would be his biggest obstacle. He prayed for the next few days, asking God to give him and his parents confidence in his decision. God answered. A few days before leaving, James overheard his dad in conversation: "Of course we are completely supportive of James going back. If James doesn't go back, the enemy will have won. He must go back to India." James couldn't believe it. He never dreamed his parents would joyfully allow him to go back, but God renewed their hearts. His parents' emotional progression from beginning to end was solely a work of the Lord. Following Christ affects two people: the one following God and the person who loves that one.

ENDNOTES

1. Todd Ahrend, *In This Generation* (Colorado Springs, CO: Dawson Media, 2010), 204.

2. Rebecca Hickman, "When Family Objects," The Traveling Team, accessed March 29, 2013, http://www.thetravelingteam.org/.

3. Norman Grubb, *C. T. Studd: Athlete and Pioneer* (Grand Rapids, MI: Zondervan, 1946), 37.

4. Hickman, "When Family Objects."

5. Courtney Anderson, *To the Golden Shore: The Life of Adoniram Judson* (Valley Forge, PA: Judson Press, 1987), 83.

Chapter Seven

No Other Name
Beliefs

I trekked north of Washington to speak in uncharted territory—Canada. I challenged the university students with verses summarizing God's heart for the world and the needs of the unreached. I exhorted them to be involved. After I finished, a member of the audience approached me. Honestly, I expected a pat on the back. I got something completely different. He said my theology was wrong and outdated. He explained, "Everyone knows those who are ignorant of the gospel will not be held accountable." I didn't know what to say. I felt nervous. The words *narrow-minded*, *rude*, and *arrogant* flashed through my head. He continued telling me that somehow, someway, those who never hear the gospel and never believe on the name of Jesus will still go to heaven. After all, how could a loving God send someone to hell? I wouldn't have been so nervous but he wasn't just any guy, he was the campus minister. Welcome to Canada!

He isn't the only one. Many have a difficult time with the doctrine of eternal punishment. A college student named John Hick wrestled with the same question. Hick was in law school when he became a believer. Once committed, he devoted much of his time to prayer, Bible study, and sharing his faith. But one thing puzzled him: the vast number of religions in the world. "If what Christianity says is true, must not what all the other world religions say be in varying degrees false? But this would mean that the large majority of mankind, consisting of everyone except the adherents of one particular religion, are walking in darkness."[1] In college I realized a majority of the West views God at the top of a mountain to which all roads ultimately lead. This isn't a Canadian thing. This is everywhere. Where did it begin?

In the 1500s, it might have been socially acceptable to say, "Outside the church there is no hope of salvation." You were either a member of the church or an atheist. The only way you would ever meet someone of a different faith is if you got on a boat, sailed around the world, and landed in a country of another religion. Today, all you have to do is walk to your local coffee shop and you'll see five different nationalities and three different religions represented. If you claim "No Christ, no hope" you will offend your Hindu, Buddhist, or Muslim neighbor. With more influence from other faiths, it's getting more controversial to have a definitive view of salvation. This is crippling for missions and a major obstacle for many Christians.[2] How do we deal with the diversity of the world and the exclusiveness of Christ?

Navigating an ocean of competing beliefs is as treacherous as the Bermuda Triangle, a legendary nautical region spanning from the island of Bermuda to the southern tip of Florida and eastward to Puerto Rico. Its coordinates form a triangle with an area of over a million square miles. Myths arose about curious incidents in this area. Ships would sail unsuspectingly into the Triangle, only to be thrown off-course and wrecked on underwater objects. Crews would go mysteriously missing. Whole fleets never heard from again.

As Christians pursue God's global mandate, many sail unknowingly into a theological Bermuda Triangle.

DEALING WITH DIVERSITY

There are three prominent philosophies one can hold in wrestling with the growing diversity in the world: pluralism, inclusivism, and exclusivism.

Many Paths. Pluralism believes all religions end up in the same place in the afterlife. Pluralists assume all will pay for their varying levels of sins, but in the end all will be brought back into right standing. Key theologians on this side of the debate are Paul Knitter and John Hick. Hick, the former law student from England, has been named as one of the twenty most influential Christian scholars.[3] In his book *God Has Many Names*, Hick says very concisely the way the apostles were speaking about Jesus was true *for the apostles.* He believes they were speaking emotionally, not definitively. Statements like "there is one mediator between God and men, the man Christ Jesus" (1 Timothy 2:5, ESV) and "there is salvation in no one else, for there is no other name under heaven given among men by which we must be saved" (Acts 4:12, ESV) are statements of emotion. These statements *describe* feelings. They are not a *prescription* for all humanity.

Knitter gives the example of a husband who says his wife is the most beautiful wife. Though several say this, all husbands can't have the most beautiful woman in the world. This is a husband's statement of love and emotion. Similarly, the way the apostles talked about Jesus was a statement of emotion to the highest degree. Knitter believes Jesus was a type of savior, not the Savior.[4] To the pluralist, God reveals Himself equally and uniquely in every culture.

Salvation is given to the Muslim through the Quran, the Hindu through Vedas and Lord Krishna, the Buddhist through the Middle Path, and the Christian through Jesus. Jesus is one of many ways to God. Pluralists will never be missional, because missions is not only irrelevant to them but also disturbing to the other revelations of God. Today, 64 percent of evangelicals and 73 percent of Protestants would classify themselves as pluralistic.[5]

The problem with pluralism is its view that God is ultimately unknowable, therefore indescribable. Since He has revealed Himself differently in every culture, all must be correct. For the pluralist, truth is everything. When everything becomes truth, nothing is truth. Stephen Prothero, professor of religious studies at Boston University, says this idea of religious pluralism is "a lovely sentiment but it is dangerous, disrespectful, and untrue.... It is time we climbed out of the rabbit hole and back to reality."[6] Any religion can prove partial truths about life and nature, because God is revealed in nature, but it is only Christ who has the answer of how a sinner can stand just before a holy God.[7]

There's a Way. The next group is inclusivism. The inclusivists affirm Jesus' crucifixion and resurrection as necessary and valuable. They believe there is "no other name under heaven ... by which we must be saved" (Acts 4:12 ESV). The uniqueness of this view is they believe it is not necessary that individuals explicitly know about Jesus. Simply put, it was essential for Jesus to die for our salvation, but it's not essential for anyone to know about the event. They believe Jesus' death paid for the sins of the world and made a way for all who submit to God. John wrote, "He is the atoning sacrifice for our sins, and not only for ours but also for the sins of the whole world" (1 John 2:2). However, inclusivists see the devotion of other religions as enough in itself. Faith in general saves, not specific knowledge and belief in Christ.

How do they justify this? They would argue that possessing faith in the religion presented to them is enough. In Saudi Arabia it's Islam. In Japan it's Buddhism. They maintain Jesus sees their faith in what they worship and accepts it as to Him. So while inclusivists do believe it is only by Jesus you can be saved, they do not believe you need to know who Jesus is to personally access grace.

A common example inclusivists use is the story of Cornelius. He was a devout, God-fearing person, yet ignorant of Christ. The book of Acts says,

> At Caesarea there was a man named Cornelius, a
> centurion of what was known as the Italian Cohort, a
> devout man who feared God with all his household,
> gave alms generously to the people, and prayed
> continually to God. About the ninth hour of the day
> he saw clearly in a vision an angel of God come in
> and say to him, "Cornelius." And he stared at him
> in terror and said, "What is it, Lord?" And he said to
> him, "Your prayers and your alms have ascended as a
> memorial before God." (Acts 10:1-4, ESV)

God was pleased by Cornelius's offerings, but how? Remember, this is before Peter arrived to explain the gospel. Inclusivists use this passage to argue the work, actions, and devotion of all those true to their religious upbringing are accepted by God. Just as Cornelius's prayers ascended to God as a memorial, so do the prayers of Muslims, Buddhists, and Hindus. They are transferred to the cross and counted as righteous. This is a monumental assumption for the fate of people who have never heard nor have access to the gospel. One I'm not willing to make.

Inclusivists must realize they fall short. Faith is a response to the work of the Holy Spirit by hearing the gospel. It is not enough to simply believe in something. Scripture makes it clear there is a direct link between salvation and knowledge of the work of Jesus on the cross. Paul said in Romans we are made righteous "through faith in Jesus Christ for all who believe" (Romans 3:22). In the book of John, the word *believe* is used over seventy times. Nearly fifty times in the New Testament *knowledge* is used, referring to explicit knowledge of the atonement of Christ. This evidence shows salvation is a work of the Lord as we respond specifically to Him. Mark states, "Repent and believe in the gospel" (Mark 1:15, ESV). Paul tells all to "repent and turn to God" (Acts 26:20). Thus, "repent and believe" is precisely what God demands of us in response to the message of Christ.

The Only Way. The third group is called exclusivism. Exclusivists, like inclusivists, believe Jesus is the only way to God. However, exclusivists believe you access this salvation when you hear the Word of God and *respond*. John says, "Whoever *believes* in the Son has eternal life; whoever does not obey the Son shall not see life, but the wrath of God remains on him" (3:36, ESV, emphasis added). Romans states, "Faith comes from hearing, and hearing through the word of Christ" (10:17, ESV). In Acts, Paul addressed a group of devout worshippers who had never heard the gospel. Paul exhorted them with specifics regarding what they must accept:

He commands all people everywhere to *repent,*
because he has fixed a day on which he will judge
the world in righteousness by a man whom he has
appointed; and of this he has given assurance to all
by raising him from the dead. (Acts 17:30-31, ESV,
emphasis added)

Those without access to the gospel, even through no
fault of their own, will spend eternity separated from God.
Wow. A difficult position, but one we must hold.

The first international student I befriended was Khalid,
a Muslim from the Middle East. As we grew closer, I really
wrestled with the question "Would Khalid really go to hell
apart from Christ?" Though he had the chance to hear
and a chance to make a decision through me sharing the
gospel with him, what about his friends and family who
would never hear the gospel? Will they be held responsible
for a message they haven't heard? What if they are true
to the faith taught to them? Thoughts of pluralism and
inclusivism sounded appealing. My internal struggle led me
to Romans 1:

Since what may be known about God is plain to
them, because God has made it plain to them.
For since the creation of the world God's invisible
qualities—his eternal power and divine nature—
have been clearly seen, being understood from what
has been made, so that people are *without excuse.*

For although they knew God, they neither
glorified him as God nor gave thanks to him, but
their thinking became futile and their foolish hearts
were darkened. (Romans 1:19-21, emphasis added)

Scripture is clear. Though everyone has some knowledge of God, no one lives up to that knowledge (v. 21). God never punishes someone for a message they've never heard. He punishes them for their sin against a holy God—a crime everyone has committed. "For all have sinned and fall short of the glory of God" (3:23). I have realized that though many people—even Christians—may embrace pluralism and inclusivism, the truest interpretation of Scripture supports exclusivism. Though I can't always comprehend it, I must embrace it.

HELL UNDER FIRE

In college, I started a conversation with one of my coworkers. He was raised to believe Jesus was the only way. However, while in high school he began questioning his beliefs. "How can an all-loving God send people to hell?" Here's an e-mail he sent me:

> Do you believe that good, loving people will go
> to hell if they do not call themselves Christians?
> What about devout Muslims or Jews? I have a hard
> time with God the punisher—at least as far as
> punishing mankind for the sin of not calling oneself
> a Christian. Where is the forgiveness in eternal
> damnation? Where is the love for His children who
> will suffer eternally?

My friend was not just questioning God but the very reality of hell itself. Is it a real place? How long would someone go there? After all, eternity is a long time.

Hell is real. It is the justice deserved for sinners against a holy God. A seminary professor once said, "Once we see the glory of Christ and the hideous nature of sin as God sees it, hell will be understandable."[8] In the attempt to downgrade hell and show a wideness in God's mercy, some not only shunned the traditional view of an everlasting hell but also tried to discredit its existence altogether. Christian authors are gaining publicity because they ask questions regarding hell, yet they give only a few vague answers that are simply misleading. Missions isn't so much about depopulating hell as it is about spreading the glory of God in Jesus. When we turn down the heat of hell we turn down the heat for the mission. Our thoughts on eternity drastically impact the way we live our lives. To make sure we stay on fire for Jesus, here are four views of this dreadful place.

View One: A Metaphor. In this view hell is not real, but invoked to scare us into better living. One advocate of this view suggests, "The problem comes when we see images in the New Testament—images that in themselves we can easily misunderstand—and then we add on a layer of our own imaginings…. Perhaps hell will be nothing like them." [9] Hell is reduced to a moral suggestion. The problem with the metaphorical view is that Jesus often refers to hell as a physical place. He warns against the wicked being thrown into Gehenna, a place known to be the city dump outside of Jerusalem. In Matthew 18:9, Jesus said, "It is better for you to enter life with one eye than to have two eyes and be thrown into the fire of hell." Viewing hell as a metaphor diminishes the seriousness of that warning. Bible scholar John Walvoord said, "The nonliteral interpretation of prophecy is largely motivated by the fact that people do not want to accept what the Bible teaches about future, especially the doctrine of punishment."[10]

View Two: A Temporary Place. This view holds to a

purgatorial role for hell. Traditionally a Catholic doctrine, it maintains hell is a place for purification of sins. Once finished, you are ready for heaven. Zachary Hayes, teacher of Catholic theology, stated,

> The notion of purgatory is intimately related to the conviction that our eternal destiny is irrevocably decided at the moment of our death and that, ultimately, our eternal destiny can be only heaven or hell. But not everyone seems "bad enough" to be consigned to an eternal hell. And most do not seem "good enough" to be candidates for heaven.... Therefore, some sort of a cleansing process is postulated between death and the entrance into heaven.[11]

The purgatorial view is largely understood in the context of Catholic Church history and has zero scriptural support. Many verses even directly oppose this view. Scripture is clear that for believers to be absent from the body is to be present with the Lord. "We know that while we are at home in the body we are away from the Lord.... and we would rather be away from the body and at home with the Lord" (2 Corinthians 5:6,8, ESV). The moralistic notion of candidates not "good enough" for heaven is contrary to the gospel. Believers have been cleansed of all unrighteousness. "We have now been justified by his blood.... While we were enemies we were reconciled to God by the death of his Son, much more, now that we are reconciled, shall we be saved by his life" (Romans 5:9-10, ESV).

View Three: We Burn Up. This view is called annihilationism. The wicked will suffer for a season and, after their payment, slowly pass out of existence. There will be no eternal, conscious punishment. Notable passages annihilationists turn to in Scripture include, "Those who are evil will be destroyed.... A little while, and the wicked *will be no more*; though you look for them, they will not be found" (Psalm 37:9-10, emphasis added). Also, "Do not be afraid of those who kill the body but cannot kill the soul. Rather, be afraid of the One who can destroy both soul and body in hell" (Matthew 10:28).

The main problem with annihilationism is the strong language in verses like Revelation 14:11: "And the smoke of their torment goes up *forever and ever*, and they have no rest, *day or night* (ESV, emphasis added)." This gives no indication the wicked will ever cease to exist, showing conclusively unbelieving persons will experience eternal, conscious torment. Supporters of annihilationism object to eternal punishment, maintaining that it is disproportionate to a finite life of sinning. However, Jonathan Edwards stated, "God is a being *infinitely* lovely, because he hath infinite excellency and beauty.... So that sin against God … must be a crime infinitely heinous, and so deserving infinite punishment."[12]

View Four: A Literal Place, Forever. Biblical scholar and theologian Richard Bauckham has said, "Until the nineteenth century almost all Christian theologians taught the reality of eternal torment in hell."[13] The traditional view is all sinners will be consciously punished for eternity. Scripture says sin must be punished: "For the wages of sin is death" (Romans 6:23). This refers to spiritual death. Hell is reserved for the punishment of sinners. "Then he will say to those on his left, 'Depart from me, you who are cursed, into the eternal fire prepared for the devil and his angels'" (Matthew 25:41). The result is those who do not know Christ will be thrown into the lake of fire. "They will be consigned to the fiery lake of burning sulfur. This is the second death" (Revelation 21:8). With a quiver in our voice we must confess hell is most assuredly everlasting and unquenchable. "And many of those who sleep in the dust of the earth shall awake, some to everlasting life, and some to shame and everlasting contempt" (Daniel 12:2, ESV). In his book *Erasing Hell*, Francis Chan stated, "There will come a day when Christ returns to reclaim His creation, and *everyone will acknowledge this*.... With this salvation and reign also comes judgment for those who opposed Christ in this life."[14]

Our "beliefs are the rails upon which our life runs," but our thoughts of eternity should never be an obstacle to living a missional life.[15] The reality of hell is a motivating factor for the kingdom of God to advance with urgency in the places it is not. What we believe about hell will dramatically impact the way we live our lives. Christ emphasized it and even died for us to avoid it. Let us not minimize it. We need to hold fast to the realities of the gospel.

In 1820 Thomas Jefferson finished compiling a new version of the Bible. It was made not by retranslating or rewriting it, but by simply removing what he didn't like. With the Bible in one hand and a knife in the other, Jefferson walked his way through the Gospels, cutting out the parts he didn't believe. Hell was one of the first to go. Prophecies, angels, miracles, the divinity of Christ, and the resurrection were next. By the time he was done, Jefferson had produced a Bible of pure ethics.

Many of us would gasp at the idea of cutting pages out

of the Bible. In reality, when we refuse to warn others about the truth of biblical teachings on hell, we are doing just what Jefferson did, removing hell.

ENDNOTES

1. John Hick, *God Has Many Names* (Philadelphia: Westminster, 1982), 17.
2. For this chapter I relied heavily on Todd Ahrend's landmark book *In This Generation* (Colorado Springs, Co: Dawson Media, 2010), as well as Timothy Tennent's *Christianity At the Religious Roundtable* (Grand Rapids, MI: Baker, 2002).
3. "The Twenty Most Influential Christian Scholars," Super Scholar, accessed March 29, 2013, http://www.SuperScholar.org.
4. Paul Knitter, *No Other Name? A Critical Survey of Christian Attitudes Toward the World Religions* (Maryknoll, NY: Orbis, 1985), 185–186.
5. "Many Christians Say Other Faiths Can Lead to Eternal Life," Pew Forum on Religion and Public Life, Dec. 18, 2008, http://www.pewforum.org/.
6. Stephen Prothero, *God Is Not One: The Eight Rival Religions That Run the World* (New York: HarperOne, 2011), 2–3.
7. Adapted from Edward John Carnell, *Christian Commitment: An Apologetic* (New York: Macmillan, 1957), viii.
8. William Crockett, ed., *Four Views on Hell* (Grand Rapids, MI: Zondervan, 1996), 48.
9. Crockett, *Four Views on Hell*, 49–50.
10. Crockett, *Four Views on Hell*, 79.
11. Crockett, *Four Views on Hell*, 99.
12. Jonathan Edwards, *The Justice of God in the Damnation of Sinners* (Minneapolis, MN: Curiosmith, 2012), 15–16.
13. Richard Bauckham, "Universalism: A Historical Survey," *Themelios* 4.2 (September 1978): 47.

14. Francis Chan and Preston M. Sprinkle, *Erasing Hell: What God Said About Eternity, and the Things We've Made Up* (Colorado Springs, CO: David C Cook, 2011), 27.
15. Dallas Willard, *The Divine Conspiracy: Rediscovering Our Hidden Life in God* (San Francisco: HarperSanFrancisco, 1998), 309.

Chapter Eight

It Seemed Good
The Call

In the late 1800s Amy Carmichael had a dream, one she remembered for her entire life. She dreamed there were dozens of blind people heading toward a perilous cliff. Amy wondered why no one tried to stop them from falling. She began calling out to them, only to produce a whisper. Off to the side, Amy noticed a peaceful group sitting, making chains of daisy flowers. When one of the group started up to help, the others pulled her back. They said, "Why should you get so excited about it? You must wait for a definite call. You haven't finished your daisy chain yet. It would be really selfish to leave us to finish the work alone." When another got up to warn them, he too was reproved, "What does it matter that these people are falling off the cliff? It has gone on for years; it will go on for years. Why make such a fuss about it?"[1] Amy Carmichael had an experience most only long for—a clear, heavenly call. Mine was a little different.

I was so ready. I was prayed up and prepared. Passport in hand. Bags packed. I was days away from heading to North Africa. Then confusion came. Someone said, "I'm so glad you've been called to ministry." I thought, *Call, what call? Did I miss it?* I was thoroughly excited and yet now uncertain.

Many Christians struggle with the mystery of a calling. The idea of a "call" is quite possibly the most confusing aspect of the journey.[2] The popular notion among Christians is to suppose there will be some sort of heavenly-vision experience. Some think an angel will flutter down into your bedroom, shake your bed, and yell, "Go to China, sucka!"[3] If that is a call, I've never had anything even similar. Most will never consider missions because they never had a call. In figuring out *if* we've been called, we first need to understand *what* a call is.

WHO'S CALLING?

The major use of the word *call* in the Bible refers to calling sinners to repentance. Peter says in the book of Acts, "The promise is for you and your children and for all who are far off—for all whom the Lord our God will call" (2:39). After the call to salvation, believers are then called to *holiness* (see 1 Thessalonians 4:7), called to *grace* (see Galatians 1:6), and called to *be saints* (see Romans 1:7, ESV). Paul was called to *be an apostle* (see Romans 1:1). Some people were called to *a specific task*, like Peter and John being called to aid in Philip's ministry in Samaria (see Acts 8:14).

As I've met with hundreds of young adults, I've realized the one thing they are looking for is to know the purpose God has for their life. "Where am I going to end up?" "What am I supposed to do?" Most are waiting for a clear voice from heaven. To bring clarity to the chaos, missions-mobilizer Paul Borthwick helps us understand the three types of callings mentioned in Scripture: the mysterious, the commissioned, and the common-sense.[4]

THE MYSTERIOUS CALL

Our most common thought when it comes to a calling is you have a mysterious dream or vision from God. Though this may happen, it is rare. This type of call finds its roots in one of Paul's journeys. As Paul was pushing the gospel through modern-day Turkey he had a vision:

> During the night Paul had a vision of a man of Macedonia standing and begging him, "Come over to Macedonia and help us." After Paul had seen the vision, we got ready at once to leave for Macedonia, concluding that God had called us to preach the gospel to them. (Acts 16:9-10)

Having seen the vision he rightly decided to go to Macedonia, where he and his coworkers eventually saw some of the first recorded converts in Europe. The vision directed the gospel from Asia to Europe.

Raymund Lull had a similar experience in the thirteenth century. His early life was marked by immorality. While in his early thirties, Lull was sitting next to his bed composing a scandalous song when he had a clear vision of Jesus on the cross. Seeing this vision repeatedly, he responded, "How can I, defiled with impurity, rise and enter in a holier life?" This experience would lead him to become a monk. While praying in the forest one day, Lull had a second vision, this time of a pilgrim. In this vision, the pilgrim scolded him for the self-centeredness of the monastic lifestyle. He left the monastery and became a missionary. He wanted to challenge European Christians to love Muslims and share the gospel with them. This was in direct contrast to the grotesque brutality of the Crusades. Lull said the conquest of the Holy Land ought to be attempted "by love and prayers and the pouring out of tears and blood."[5] He founded a monastery to train up missionaries while successfully convincing universities to teach Arabic. Lull held fast to the end of his life. He was martyred in Algeria by the very people he was trying to reach. Indeed, he was a product of a mysterious call!

THE COMMISSIONED CALL

The second type of call Borthwick names is the commissioned call. This is where the leadership of the church, guided by the Holy Spirit, exhorts you to go. An example of this is given in Acts:

> Now there were in the church at Antioch prophets
> and teachers.... While they were worshiping the
> Lord and fasting, the Holy Spirit said, "Set apart for
> me Barnabas and Saul for the work to which I have
> called them." Then after fasting and praying they
> laid their hands on them and sent them off. (Acts
> 13:1-3, ESV)

Paul and Barnabas were called by the Holy Spirit through the church leaders to a specific task. The difference between the mysterious call and the commissioned call is the vision comes to the leaders, not the individual. Though this call seems unusual, it isn't as astonishing as it may seem. The church leaders were asking the Lord to speak to them. When they heard from God to set apart Paul and Barnabas, the leadership concluded the church was to commission these believers to proclaim the gospel to new areas.

In the 1400s, a man named Jon Hus started teaching

the Bible to a group of people in Bohemia (modern-day eastern Czech Republic).[6] Hus was martyred for teaching the Bible, but before his death he declared there would be a movement after him that his persecutors wouldn't be able to stop. Nearly 200 years later, Bishop John Amos Comenius was teaching the Bible in Moravia (modern-day western Czech Republic) to a group of believers that could trace their faith to Hus's influence. Comenius too was martyred for his actions but before his death he declared there was a hidden seed in these Moravians that would spring up in revival in 100 years. In the early 1700s, Nikolaus von Zinzendorf took a single Moravian refugee into his estate in Herrnhut. Before long, Zinzendorf had several hundred Moravians living on his land. He led the Moravians in reading the Word and prayer. On August 12, 1727, Zinzendorf called a prayer meeting to celebrate Hus's prophecy. This meeting ignited a revival, and the Moravians committed to pray twenty-four hours a day. This lasted 110 years! Unsurprisingly, throughout these years of prayer the Moravian Church commissioned a great number of missionaries. Some went trusting their leaders who heard from the Holy Spirit to send them out. The commissioned call is just as viable as the mysterious call.

COMMON-SENSE CALL

The third type of call is the common-sense call. At the beginning of Acts Christianity was seen as a small Jewish sect. By Acts 15 many people were turning to Christ, including non-Jews (Gentiles). Because of this, Jewish Christians were forming opinions regarding the Gentiles' salvation. Should the Gentiles submit to Old Testament law before becoming a Christian? What requirements did they need to adhere to? In light of this argument among believers, the apostles and elders met. They concluded God cleanses the heart of the believer the same way for everyone, regardless of culture. The church needed to send men from the council to share the news with believers in other areas. Was there a mysterious call? No. A commissioned call? No. Here is how they decided: "*It seemed good ... to choose men from among them and send them to Antioch*" (Acts 15:22, ESV, emphasis added). There was a need for a messenger, and there were people willing to go. It appears there are times it will just seem good to meet the need.

Jesus likened the leading of the Holy Spirit to wind (see John 3:8). When we understand the different types of callings, we can be like sailors who open our sails. We move forward in obedience to God, pursuing His purpose and navigating our life in the direction of His leading. The question we must ask is, "Are our sails open?" Are we allowing God to lead us by all the different types of calls, or are we relying on just one?

WHAT'S WRONG HERE?

Inevitably, there will be times we have opened our lives to God's leading but don't seem to be hearing anything. What should we do when there seems to be no wind?

The first time I went sailing was on Lake Union in Seattle. As we boarded the ship, our fearless leader, Captain John, opened the sails. Within minutes we were in the middle of the lake. My eyes were closed and the wind in my face. I was loving every minute. Everything was perfect until I realized our boat was slowing. No more wind.

I'm not one to jump to extremes, but we were stranded in the middle of a lake. Without blinking, the captain grabbed a long piece of wood, thrust it into my hands, and yelled, "Paddle!" So much for sailing.

If we survey the church today, most would say they have never had a mysterious call to missions. Which is fine. If we probe deeper we find what they mean is they have never had a God-given attraction to a specific country. We, like Abraham, get to step out in obedience to follow Jesus regardless of where He takes us (see Genesis 12:3-4). Though I've never heard the voice of God or had a mysterious liver-quiver, I have grown to understand people may be *called* to live a missional life simply because they understand what God is doing and desire to join Him. They paddle in obedience to God's mission.

Today, millions lack access to the gospel. We must not feel the need to be stagnant until we hear a word from the Lord, a vision, or a "call." For some, it might just *seem good* to send people where no one is going.

The common-sense call is logical, but just because there is a need doesn't mean we should rush in with no preparation. "Desire without knowledge is not good—how much more will hasty feet miss the way!" (Proverbs 19:2). Ignoring cautions, failing to train, and going rogue will set you up for disaster. "Plans fail for lack of counsel, but with many advisers they succeed" (15:22). Seeking wise counsel is crucial when navigating the call.

No two people are alike—in life and in their personal relationship with God. Why do we reduce the entrance into God's mission to a single mysterious experience? In Scripture, God communicates uniquely with people to accomplish His purposes. The call to missions is no different.

PLEASE SEND SOMEONE ELSE

I struggled with the thought of being a missionary. I saw missionaries as a select few God had called to wear a loincloth. As I saw God's plan through Scripture, I realized missionaries are normal Christians who love the Lord and want to see His glory spread to all people groups. The loincloths are optional. The lack of a calling is no reason to never get involved. Though this may be our obstacle, at times there is something deeper behind our inactivity. In Exodus, God sends Moses to free Israel from the bondage of Pharaoh. In these few verses, observe how many times God refers to Himself:

> Then the Lord said, "*I* have surely seen the affliction of *my* people who are in Egypt and have heard their cry because of their taskmasters. *I* know their sufferings, and *I* have come down to deliver them out of the hand of the Egyptians and to bring them up out of that land to a good and broad land.... Behold, the cry of the people of Israel has come to *me*, and *I* have also seen the oppression with which the Egyptians oppress them. Come, *I* will send you to Pharaoh that you may bring *my* people, the children of Israel, out of Egypt." (Exodus 3:7-10, ESV, emphasis added)

Eight times God points out it is not about Moses and not even about Israel, it's about Him. God set His ultimate purpose to be His desire. Moses's response? "Who am I that I should go?" (v. 11). Just like Moses, we ask, "Who am I?" and focus on our lack of abilities instead of the fullness of God's.

God says to Moses, "I will be with you" (v. 12). He gives Moses and us assurance, "It's not about you. It's about Me."

In Exodus 4, Moses shows the heart issue. He begs God, "Please send someone else" (v. 13). When we are honest with ourselves, the issue is not in believing God can use us, but that He *will* use us. We are afraid of the uncertainties of a radical life. In the words of Paul Fleming, founder of New Tribes Mission, "Here am I, Lord ... send my sister."[7]

I have found people will use the lack of a mysterious call as an excuse to not be involved. We must realize God uses more than one type of call. May we be open to how God directs us.

ANSWERING THE CALL

We can all see if anyone was *called* to be a missionary it was the apostle Paul. In the beginning of Acts, he was well known around the Roman Empire as Saul, the persecutor of the church. Then he met Jesus.

> As [Saul] neared Damascus on his journey, suddenly a light from heaven flashed around him. He fell to the ground and heard a voice say to him, "Saul, Saul, why do you persecute me?" "Who are you, Lord?" Saul asked. "I am Jesus, whom you are persecuting," he replied. "Now get up and go into the city, and you will be told what you must do." (Acts 9:3-6)

After appearing to the man soon to be known as Paul, Jesus spoke to Ananias to tell him what to do when Paul arrived:

> The Lord told him, "Go to the house of Judas on Straight Street and ask for a man from Tarsus named

Saul.... This man is my chosen instrument to
proclaim my name to the Gentiles and their kings
and to the people of Israel." (vv. 11,15)

God confirmed Paul's calling. The Lord said, "I am
sending you to ... open their eyes and turn them from
darkness to light, and from the power of Satan to God, so
that they may receive forgiveness of sins and a place among
those who are sanctified by faith in me" (26:17-18).

God called Paul to carry the gospel to those who do not
have it. In Romans Paul stated he had fulfilled this mission
in that particular area. Then he moved on to further parts
of the world where the gospel was not. Paul didn't point
to the encounter with Jesus, the calling of Jesus, or the
commission of Jesus. Paul said,

> So from Jerusalem all the way around to Illyricum,
> I have fully proclaimed the gospel of Christ. It
> has always been my ambition to preach the gospel
> where Christ was not known, so that I would not be
> building on someone else's foundation.
> (Romans 15:19-20)

Then Paul quoted from Isaiah, "Rather, as it is written:
'Those who were not told about him will see, and those who
have not heard will understand'" (v. 21; Isaiah 52:15). Paul
continued,

> This is why I have often been hindered from coming
> to you. But now that there is no more place for me
> to work in these regions, and since I have been

longing for many years to visit you, I plan to do so
when I go to Spain. (Romans 15:22-24)

His reason for taking the gospel to new areas was an
Old Testament promise: Jesus will be worshipped among
those who have never heard. Paul never pointed back to
his vision of the man from Macedonia. For our benefit, he
pointed to the larger picture of spreading the gospel. We
don't need a call to be involved in God's mission.[8] Scripture
clearly states we all have a part to play. To hold fast in
obedience we open our sails, and when necessary paddle,
toward God's purpose.

ENDNOTES

1. Amy Carmichael, "Amy Carmichael's Dream," The Traveling Team, accessed March 29, 2013, http://www.thetravelingteam.org/.

2. J Herbert Kane, *Understanding Christian Missions* (Grand Rapids, MI: Baker, 1982), 39.

3. Brad Buser, missionary and cofounder of Radius International, was the first to share this with me.

4. Paul Borthwick, "The Call to Missions," in Steve Hoke and Bill Taylor, *Global Mission Handbook: A Guide for Crosscultural Service* (Downers Grove, IL: InterVarsity, 2009), 67.

5. Samuel M. Zwemer, *Raymund Lull: First Missionary to the Moslems* (New York: Funk & Wagnalls, 1902), 53.

6. "A Brief History of the Moravian Church." The Moravian Church in North America, accessed April 8, 2013, http://www.Moravian.org/.

7. Paul Fleming, "Here Am I, Send My Sister," The Traveling Team, accessed March 29, 2013, http://www.thetravelingteam.org/.

8. Inspired by John Piper, *A Holy Ambition: To Preach Where Christ Has Not Been Named* (Minneapolis, MN: Desiring God, 2011), 18.

Chapter Nine

The Lender's Slave
Debt

Nathan was an outstanding student. He was involved in sports, a fraternity, a part-time job, and even Bible study. He mentored guys on campus and spent time with internationals. Upon graduation, he wanted to do something incredible with his life. He wanted to be a missionary. One thing stood in his way: $25,000 in student loans.

Some people are fortunate to be debt-free. For most, debt seems synonymous with the American lifestyle. Debt is spending money you don't have. Biblically, Christians are to be channels of blessings. Psalms says, "May God be gracious to us and bless us and make his face shine on us" (67:1). This is not a psalm about simply receiving God's blessings. We must ask why God wants to bless us? The psalm continues, "That your ways may be known on earth, your salvation among all nations" (v. 2). Everything God does is focused on bringing Him glory, even when He blesses us. We must ask ourselves, "How am I stewarding God's blessings?"

THE THREAT OF DEBT
The majority of people walk a fine line regarding debt. For Christians the stakes are high. It is a major obstacle to fulfilling

the Great Commission. It affects how much we give and whether we are free to go. I'm not able to step out in faith when I am miles deep in debt. It can sideline you from ministry. It's an issue for anyone desiring to play a role in world evangelization, regardless of geography or vocation. The simple reality is consumer debt is a threat greater than we imagine. One financial adviser observed, "I have known people who have not been able to go on the mission field because of debt. Going is their intention, but unfortunately life happens. They start off working hard to get the loan paid off, but end up with more obligations and ties as time rolls on."[1]

Those who pay no attention to debt will suffer an increasingly difficult work schedule, a spiraling downward of relationships, and very difficult home life. The bondage and burden of debt is overwhelming. Seventy-one percent of Americans say debt makes their home lives unhappy, and more than half the people in the US stress heavily over their financial situation.[2] It's no coincidence the number one reason for divorce in the US is money![3]

Based on the way the public talks about loans, mortgages, and debt, it seems we think banks are pure in their intent. Most people would not be deceived by overt ploys of salesmen in a business, but surprisingly people walk into a bank, take out a loan, and thinking the bank has their best interests at heart. Banks are not nonprofit organizations. They too need to make money. Your loan is their interest!

However, banks look like saints compared to credit card companies. Every college freshman can fill out credit card paperwork and walk away with a free water bottle, having no idea they are on the brink of disaster. Businesses know human beings have the capacity to learn to want almost any conceivable material object.[4] This is why there are over fifteen billion credit advertisement impressions on the American public every three months![5] One can say no most of the time. Eventually, however, I will give in and buy the new jumping alarm clock. No wonder the average American household with debt has nearly $16,000 of it.[6] The average college senior possesses six credit cards, and their balance is between $3,000 and $7,000![7] This year, student loan debt topped one trillion dollars, the highest in history.[8]

Debt causes stress, tension, and an unnecessary burden. Paul said, "It is for freedom that Christ has set us free. Stand firm, then, and do not let yourselves be burdened again by a yoke of slavery" (Galatians 5:1). God's intent is for believers to use their blessings for His kingdom, but being in debt can make us slaves to ours.

BLESSING OR BONDAGE

While traveling through Moorhead, Minnesota, I toured the *Hjemkomst* (pronounced "Yom-komst," it means "homecoming"). A junior high school counselor built this replica Viking ship in the 1970s. In 1982, the *Hjemkomst* made an epic journey, sailing Lake Superior, across the Atlantic Ocean, and on to Norway. Dating back to AD 800, the Vikings of Scandinavia developed an innovative ship that gave them a strategic advantage over the military might of the great Charlemagne, leader of the Holy Roman Empire. The design? The ships were large enough to take on the ocean, yet shallow enough to float the smallest rivers. In light of this, the Vikings were able to sail further inland than any other oceangoing vessel. However, the change came at a price. The boats were shallow and small, only big enough for the crew and necessary supplies. This drastically limited what they could store on board. There was no room for extra cargo. As we hold fast to God's mission, we want to be wise with our cargo. Debt is burdensome. It is excessive cargo. To hold fast to the mission, we must dump the debt.

At a restaurant in Tennessee, I started talking with my waiter, a college graduate from a private university in the northeast. His tuition totaled $100,000. Unable to find a job in his field, he had to work two jobs to make payments on his loans. Unfortunately his situation is becoming normal. Higher education is a great choice, but it frequently creates higher debt.

I often hear people say, "I would love to work in ministry, I just can't." We have become consumed with managing our blessings. I've known many whom God has blessed with incredible families, large houses, good jobs, excellent health, or even some money in the bank, yet they find themselves in bondage. Blessings will become bondage when they become our focus.

From a global perspective, many Americans are blessed with affluence. America is one of the wealthiest nations in history. Yet ironically 53 percent of Christians haven't given to their church in the past month.[9] Add to this, total giving hasn't risen above 3 percent of church members' income in the past forty years.[10] It may not be that Christians *don't* give, it may be they *can't* give. As believers, somewhere inside of us there is a desire to give generously. Two-thirds of Americans live paycheck to paycheck.[11] How is that? It doesn't help that the average American spends 95 percent of their income, leaving little to save. For every hundred dollars we make, we spend all but five. We don't get involved in kingdom ministry because we live in a prison of debt.

Ralph Winter, cofounder of the US Center for World Mission, said, "Most evangelical families are so terribly in debt that there's no possibility they will change their pattern of consumption in any significant way."[12] We have managed to make debt look normal, even appealing. However, Scripture clearly warns about debt: "The rich rules over the poor, and the borrower becomes the lender's slave" (Proverbs 22:7, NASB). Slavery might be a strong term, but a slave has no freedom. Debt robs you of your freedom. A slave is tied to his master the same as a borrower is bound to his debt. Debt will own you. Your free time will be gone to second and third jobs. It will command your family and ministry time. A master rules over a slave like debt rules over the debtor. Once we see our debt robs us of freedom, we begin to see the seriousness of it. Our tendency is to buy everything with borrowed money. Spending money you don't have on clothes and vacations, gadgets and grills, has made debt a way of life.

Jesus said, "No one can serve two masters, for either he will hate the one and love the other, or he will be devoted to the one and despise the other. You cannot serve God and money" (Matthew 6:24, ESV). Debt is demanding. Jesus makes the issue less a matter of money and more a matter of our heart. Unmanaged debt keeps us from serving the true Master.

So is it wrong to have nice things? Not at all. Taking a family vacation or driving a quality car isn't sin, just as living in poverty doesn't make someone holy. After all, there can be more pride in poverty than in riches. Praying about our spending is an important discipline. Many have heard the saying, "Money is the root of all evil," but that isn't biblical. Scripture actually says, "The *love* of money is a root of *all kinds* of evil" (1 Timothy 6:10, emphasis added). The focus is taken off the evilness of money and attributed to the heart of the spender. Money is neither moral nor immoral; it's amoral. That means it lies outside the boundaries of morality. It can be used for good or bad. Morality, then, is ascribed by our intentions. The way we spend our money reflects our heart. As Jesus said, "Where your treasure is, there your heart will be also" (Matthew 6:21). Look at the way you spend your money; it will reveal what is important to you.

ARE YOU HEALTHY?

The best way to stay out of debt is to not spend money you don't have. Simple principle. Hard to follow. Financial planner Chris Haas stated, "People are spending more money than they are taking in, and they are doing this because they can. They can get a credit card. They can go to the store and get a payment plan. They can get it now and they don't have to wait."

Every situation is different. There are times it is appropriate to borrow money. Here is a principle to consider. There are two types of debt: healthy and unhealthy. Instead of trying to *prescribe* what is good and bad, it is more helpful to *describe* examples:

> Healthy: Going to college and taking out some student loans.

> Unhealthy: Taking out student loans and using money to buy stuff. Then dropping out of college.

> Healthy: Taking on a mortgage for a home within your income range.

Unhealthy: Buying a house and not having adequate income.

Healthy: Using a credit card with a reasonable interest rate to pay for items you budget.

Unhealthy: Always needing the latest gadgets, so you charge them with money you don't have.

For a deeper heart check, here is some helpful advice to serve as a guideline for making purchases:

1. Ask yourself, "What are my motives in buying this product?" If you are trying to keep in step with the latest fashion or improve your self-esteem, maybe that purchase isn't the best idea.
2. Wait and pray forty-eight hours. If at all possible, wait before making a purchase to avoid impulse buying. The larger the investment, the longer we need to think about the purchase.
3. Seek counsel before you purchase. If you are married, ask your spouse. Go to someone you respect for the way they spend their money and ask them if it is a wise purchase.
4. Stay away from plastic! Have a healthy fear of credit cards. They are dangerous because of the fine print and lack of accountability. If you absolutely need a card for purchases, use a debit card. The scary part is the more we use a card, the easier it is to purchase things. Because we don't actually see the money leaving our pocket, we don't feel the emotion like we do with cash.
5. For the recent graduate, don't try to mimic well-established, older people. The way they are living their life is a product of many years of income and sacrifices.

Very few people will have a stable, affluent lifestyle directly out of college. Don't pretend to be the exception. Pretending in the real world with real money and real consequences is a recipe for disaster.

Debt is not the end of the world. If you have debt, don't be dismayed. Get accountability and realize there is hope. Live within your means and develop a plan to get out of debt. You will need to sacrifice temporary pleasures and discipline yourself for the long-term goal. We have to guard ourselves from the trap of our culture that says we need the newest technology and the latest fashion or we are obsolete. In reality if you commit to a plan, your debt will be the thing that's obsolete!

It is helpful to remember the longer we wait to pay off our debt, the more interest we accrue. In the end we will pay significantly more than we originally borrowed. Take Nathan, for example. If he graduates with $25,000 of loans he will be tempted to pay the minimum monthly payments. For Nathan that is roughly $290 a month for ten years. With interest, he would pay a total of $34,500, nearly $10,000 more! On the other hand, if Nathan pays a little more each month—say $500—he would save five years and nearly $5,000. Nathan could live simply and make huge progress, or pay double.

TO TITHE OR NOT TO TITHE

In the Old Testament, the Israelites were required to give 10 percent of their income as an offering to the Lord (see Leviticus 27:30-33). Interestingly, the New Testament model doesn't command a percentage of giving. The standard is simply to give generously and cheerfully.

"Each one must give as he has decided in his heart, not reluctantly or under compulsion, for God loves a cheerful giver" (2 Corinthians 9:7, ESV). We are to give joyfully and voluntarily because everything we have is a gift from God. By tithing, we recognize our dependence on God to supply everything we need and we show gratitude to God for the things He's given.

In 2 Corinthians, Paul admired the churches of Macedonia because they gave "according to their ability, and beyond their ability" (2 Corinthians 8:3, NASB). They begged Paul to let them give so they could be a part of what God was doing (see v. 4), even at times out of their extreme poverty. Whether we give 10 percent or 90 percent, we should always give in a voluntary, joyful manner. Believers should ask God how He would have them give. The standard of giving is not found in a percentage, but in the example of Christ: "For you know the grace of our Lord Jesus Christ, that though he was rich, yet for your sake He became poor, so that you through his poverty might become rich" (v. 9).

A huge mistake is to think we don't have money because we don't have *a lot* of money. What happens when you find yourself with two options: tithe or pay the bills? This is difficult. There are two views on how to handle this situation.

The first view is to continue tithing 10 percent. Though it will be incredibly tough, the thought is if we give 10 percent God will bless our 90 percent. In Malachi, God says, "Bring the whole tithe into the storehouse, that there may be food in my house. Test me in this … and see if I will not throw open the floodgates of heaven and pour out so much blessing that there will not be room enough to store it" (Malachi 3:10). Tithing is an outward expression of our faith in God to provide for us.

The second view is to at least give some. Giving a little is better than giving nothing. Give what you can, as you can. Set goals and live a simpler lifestyle. The gospel of Mark tells the story of a widow who gave two coins. Jesus saw her giving and told the disciples, "This poor widow has put in more than all those who are contributing to the offering box" (Mark 12:43, ESV). The widow joyfully gave the little she had, and Jesus commended her faith. Tithing teaches us to always put God first in our lives and reminds us that everything we have belongs to God.

A SURE WAY

Many are looking for the golden ticket to financial freedom. I have actually found it. It's called a budget! The only way you can be certain of freedom from debt is to have a budget for your expenses. Find out where your money is going. There are many systems in place to aid you in a financial plan. We just need to get one. The majority of Americans have financial problems because the majority of Americans don't budget.

Everything in you will want to buck the budget. At times it feels oppressive, even demeaning. It feels like getting an allowance all over again. However, when we fully realize the burden of debt and the blessing of financial freedom, we see a budget as a catalyst to help us, and no longer as a burden. Controlling debt enables us to live a more missional life. Budgeting is a great example of how to hold fast. Dump the debt and sail freely.

I have always despised budgeting. I remember as I was growing up my parents would portion out my allowance in short-term, long-term, and tithing. My method of saving was putting coins in a jar and spending the long-term on the things that would last, like Legos. So much for long-term perspective. It wasn't until my final year of college I began realizing budgeting was a big deal. I took a class on personal finances. It opened my eyes to the harsh realities of the financial world. I met with a financial adviser who put me on a spending plan and helped me pay off my loans. By spending less each month on frivolous things and applying a little more each month to my student loans, I was able to get out of debt in half the time and even started a savings account. Budgeting isn't always fun. In the moment, it's hard to say no to the temptations. Yet, in the end, smart financial decisions free you. By believing one day I will be free, I've been able to see the blessing has far outweighed the sacrifice.

THE AVERAGE COUPLE

Laura and Sam both had expensive tastes and spent much of their early marriage accumulating debt. Before long, they knew they needed help. A financial class was starting at their church. Sam mentioned it to Laura to help her. She agreed because she knew it would help him! After the first class they were both stunned. For the first time it sank in—they were $50,000 in debt, and this didn't include their student loans or mortgage. "Surely we're hopeless," Laura thought. Sam earned a modest salary and Laura worked a job she hated. They both felt there was no way out. Laura started visualizing food stamps and working into her nineties!

Over the next six weeks their paradigm shifted as discipline entered their budget. She said, "I'd like to tell you we were 100 percent disciplined, did everything we were told, and prayed about it every day. Truth be told we went to all six of our financial planning classes and did the best of our ability." Once their spending plan was in place they started paying down their debt. Getting out of debt became their top priority. "Paying off debt became an obsession. It's amazing how fast budgeting works."

Three years later Laura became a stay-at-home mom. They are down to their last $3,000 in debt. Even though they can see financial freedom within reach, Sam and Laura still meet with their financial adviser and use a cash management system. Laura now holds this motto, "Work more, spend less, and sell stuff." Here's a couple with limited income, and they overcame. So can you!

ENDNOTES

1. Chris Haas, president of Freedom5:one Ministries. Most of this section was inspired by Dave Ramsey's book *Financial Peace Revisited* (New York: Viking, 2003), and by Chris Haas, president of Freedom 5:one Ministries, a nonprofit financial counseling organization, http://freedom5one.com/.

2. Ramsey, *Financial Peace Revisited*, 9.

3. Elizabeth Bernstein, "Divorce's Guide to Marriage: Study Reveals Five Common Themes Underlie Most Divorces," *Wall Street Journal*, July 24, 2012, http://online.wsj.com/.

4. Timothy Ferriss, *The 4-Hour Workweek: Escape 9-5, Live Anywhere, and Join the New Rich* (New York: Crown, 2007), 243.

5. Ramsey, *Financial Peace Revisited*, 11.

6. Ben Woolsey and Matt Schulz, "Credit Card Statistics, Industry Facts, Debt Statistics," February 28, 2012, http://www.creditcards.com/.

7. Fred Gabriel, "Educating College Students about Debt," March 4, 2012, http://www.investmentnews.com/.

8. Josh Mitchell and Maya Jackson-Randall, *Student-Loan Debt Tops $1 Trillion*, March 22, 2012, http://online.wsj.com/.

9. Available from http://www.daveramsey.com/.

10. Available from http://www.daveramsey.com/.

11. Jim Forsyth, "More Than Two-Thirds in US Live Paycheck to Paycheck," September 19, 2012, http://www.reuters.com/.

12. Amy Prange, "Debt," The Traveling Team, accessed March 29, 2013, http://www.thetravelingteam.org/.

Chapter Ten

Worthy of the Wage
Support Raising

The Great Wall is the largest man-made structure in the world. It stretches over four thousand miles across China's northern border. For centuries, the wall protected China from foreign invasions. However, in 1644, the Great Wall didn't stop the Northern Manchu tribe from invading China. What was their strategy? They walked through the door. The Manchurians persuaded a Ming general to unlock the gate, and the 276-year Ming Dynasty came to an end.

We look at obstacles and see where others have failed. We become fearful to face the same issues. Though something may look insurmountable, there are ways to overcome. When it comes to ministry, many look at support raising and see the Great Wall.

Support raising takes preparation, and it doesn't come naturally. While speaking at a college in Montana, I met a student who was convinced he wasn't called to missions. Why? He couldn't raise his support. He gave up on God's global plan because of money! An improper view of support raising has major ramifications. From the beginner to the experienced, support raising can get the best of us. Because raising support is an obstacle, excuses emerge quickly. The truth is support raising is not unbiblical, it is simply un-American.

The Age of Discovery was the period in the early fifteenth century when Europeans started exploring the New World. Land routes going east would no longer suffice, and exploration ships were sent in every direction to find new routes to Asia. Christopher Columbus believed Asia was more quickly reached by sailing west from Europe, as opposed to around the southern tip of Africa. It was here Columbus found America, and the Age of Discovery came to full force with one intention—colonization of the New World. Longing to conquer the Americas, kingdoms would send out explorers. Though some sailors funded their own way through the business of shipping, most had their journeys financed by an empire.

In the book of John, Jesus claims nearly forty times to be "sent" from God. The final time He says, "As the Father has sent me, I am sending you" (John 20:21). As believers, we are commissioned by the kingdom of heaven. God's mission is our order. As His sent ones, we depend on His kingdom to fund the mission.

MAKING TENTS

One of the most common arguments against support raising revolves around making tents. Paul the apostle was a tentmaker by trade (see Acts 18:3). He stated, "You remember, brothers and sisters, our toil and hardship; we worked night and day in order not to be a burden to anyone while we preached the gospel of God to you" (1 Thessalonians 2:9). While Paul was in Thessalonica he chose to work as a tentmaker so he would not burden them with supporting him while he ministered. Some today have adopted this as their philosophy. They are quick to dismiss support raising in favor of being a "tentmaker," also known as bivocational ministry. This model revolves around working full-time for income while also doing ministry. By working his trade, Paul was seemingly able to make, repair, and sell tents in such a way that it was profitable enough to supply his needs.

Though there is a place for this model, it is important to realize this was by no means normal for Paul. There were times when he chose to have his income from tent making, but this was temporary. Acts says, "When Silas and Timothy came from Macedonia, Paul devoted himself exclusively to preaching, testifying to the Jews that Jesus was the Messiah" (18:5). When Silas and Timothy joined Paul they brought with them support from churches in Macedonia. In light of this support, the missionaries were able to dedicate themselves fully to the gospel. Paul not only raised support, he was in a partnership with churches for support. He did not make use of this with some churches, but he explained to them he had every right to earn pay from his ministry. He said, "If we have sown spiritual things among you, is it too much if we reap material things from you? If others share this rightful claim on you, do not we even more?" (1 Corinthians 9:11-12, ESV). Paul compared his ministry work with farmers, shepherds, and soldiers (see 9:7). He argued everyone is paid for their work, and so should full-time ministers be.

It could be that the country you desire to minister in requires strategic access. In this case, to establish residency "tent making," or finding a job in your field of experience, may be the only option. Keep in mind the majority of those who do choose this model will still raise some support. This is because the countries they work in are unable to pay a salary for the worker to live at an adequate lifestyle.

DON'T MUZZLE THE OX

Paul wasn't the only person who raised support. Jesus did too. Luke tells us that in addition to the disciples, some women traveled with Him:

> Mary (called Magdalene) from whom seven demons had come out; Joanna the wife of Chuza, the manager of Herod's household; Susanna; and many others. These women *were helping to support them* out of their own means. (Luke 8:2-3, NIV)

Various women and others provided for Jesus and the disciples. Jesus depended on them for support while doing ministry. He commissioned the disciples to do their ministry empty-handed, reminding them, "The laborer is worthy of his wages" (10:7, NASB). For this reason, Peter and other apostles lived on the gifts and donations of the church so they could dedicate themselves wholly to ministry. Acts says, "All who believed were together and had all things in common," and "there was not a needy person among them, for as many as were owners of lands or houses sold them and brought the proceeds of what was sold" (2:44; 4:34, ESV). All of this was going on while the apostles were devoted "to prayer and to the ministry of the word" (6:4, ESV).

This is not just a New Testament concept. It began in the Old Testament. Forty years after leaving Egypt, Joshua led Israel into the Promised Land. The land was split and given to the tribes of Israel, but the tribe of Levi was not given a portion like the others. Each tribe was to give the Levites 10 percent of their portion. The Lord said, "To the Levites I have given every tithe in Israel for an inheritance, in return for their service that they do, their service in the tent of meeting" (Numbers 18:21, ESV). Why? So the Levites could be fully given to the work of God.

Old Testament law said, "Do not muzzle an ox while it is treading out the grain" (Deuteronomy 25:4). Most of us have never been farmers and fewer have muzzled an ox, so how do we make sense of this verse? When you muzzle an ox its mouth is covered so, in this case, it cannot eat. When an animal works hard but cannot eat, it does not work efficiently. Paul used this concept in discussing support raising:

> Is it for oxen that God is concerned? Does he not certainly speak for our sake? It was written for our sake, because the plowman should plow in hope and the thresher thresh in hope of sharing in the crop.... The Lord commanded that those who proclaim the gospel should get their living by the gospel.
> (1 Corinthians 9:9-10,14, ESV)

This serves as a reminder for us. Just as oxen get fed, farmers get their crop, and soldiers get provisions, so too workers of the gospel should receive their income by the gospel.

RAISING AWARENESS

The main reason people don't financially invest in things is because they have never been asked. Support raising is not just for the receiver but the giver as well. When we ask people to get involved with our ministry we make known our need and rally others to the cause. We are not only raising money but raising awareness.

In 444 BC Nehemiah was the cupbearer to the king of

Persia. Two travelers from Israel came through and informed Nehemiah his homeland was in ruins. He wept for days and pleaded with God to grant him mercy from the king (see Nehemiah 1:11). Nehemiah was going to ask the king for his support. Can you imagine how intimidating this would be? Nehemiah, a foreigner, in the presence of a pagan king. The king's response could have been anything. Nehemiah boldly requested, "Send me to the city in Judah where my ancestors are buried so that I can rebuild it" (2:5). Incredibly, the king fulfilled all of Nehemiah's needs and more (see vv. 8-9). By the end, Nehemiah had rallied the whole nation of Israel to rebuild the wall of Jerusalem, finishing his task.

When we are able to invite people around the ultimate vision, we allow them to be a part of what God is doing. Raising support allows us to recruit a small army of pray-ers, suppliers, and resourcers to help accomplish the purpose God has given us. Paul modeled this well. He wrote the Philippians, saying,

> And you Philippians yourselves know that in the beginning of the gospel, when I left Macedonia, no church entered into partnership with me in giving and receiving, except you only. Even in Thessalonica you sent me help for my needs once and again. *Not that I seek the gift, but I seek the fruit that increases to your credit.* I have received full payment, and more. (Philippians 4:15-18, ESV, emphasis added)

Not only did he get resources from the believers in Philippi, he helped them get involved!

My friend Aaron went on staff with a ministry and started raising support. While sharing the vision to a small

Bible study, Aaron met Jeff. Jeff was so overwhelmed he not only joined for a monthly investment, but he got others involved. He didn't stop there. As Jeff started giving to Aaron, God started stirring his heart to do more than give; he was moved to go. A year to the day Jeff started giving to Aaron, Jeff was in the mission field! Raising support is not just about you, it's a way to get others involved in God's plan for the nations.

Make no mistake. You are not a second-class Christian if you stay and support the goers. King David established a principle in Israelite warfare, "The share of the man who stayed with the supplies is to be the same as that of him who went down to the battle. All will share alike" (1 Samuel 30:24). You are just as valuable and needed if you stay to supply the front lines with resources. We all have a part in the mission of spreading the gospel, whether you are a goer or a giver.

REAL FEARS

In college I ran across a job opportunity that seemed perfect. The job description read, "Students needed to do office duties, editing and revising missions material for publication, make your own hours, great pay." I couldn't think of a better job to work around my schedule. My interview went well, and I landed the job. However, my enthusiasm waned when they said my salary was based on the support I raised. I thought, "What kind of scam is this?" Upon graduation I went into full-time ministry. Guess what? I had to raise my own support. I wanted to say no. I thought it was a burden, and I thought I would fail. Support raising is a never-ending cycle: seeking contacts, requesting referrals, making the initial phone calls, asking for money.

I was freaking out over the idea, so I sought advice from a friend who had lived on support for over two decades. He asked, "If you could have any job in the world and the pay was sufficient, what job would you want?" As I thought about the question I realized I wanted to work in ministry. I wanted to point people to Jesus. He said, "Don't let something as small as money stand in your way." Paradigm shift.

People fear support raising for many reasons. Some see their lack of contacts, some fear rejection, some failure, others debt. When we begin raising support, fears run rampant. But how should we handle them?

Contacts. When Allison started raising support, she made a list of potential support contacts with whom to share the vision of her ministry. Growing up in a small town, her list was mostly family and church friends. Allison was encouraged at first, but within two months she exhausted every contact and was only halfway to her goal. Her initial encouragement was replaced with anxiety. What would she do? Should she stop? Retreat? Cry?

When faced with this problem we can either quit or get strategic. Allison got strategic. She thought beyond her church and family: doctors, hairstylists, pharmacists, teachers, and coaches. Who else would want to be involved in her ministry? She went to her initial list and asked for referrals. Allison not only reached her support goal, but was able to introduce God's vision for the nations to dozens of people.

Rejection. In support raising, irrational thoughts creep in fast. *Will people think I'm begging? What if they say no? Will they de-friend me? Will this ruin our friendship?*

Columbus was persistent. Before he set sail, he presented

his vision to multiple kingdoms. He was rejected every time. The Crown of Castile eventually took him up on his proposal, but not on the first occasion Columbus cast his vision to them. The first time, they turned him down, stating Columbus was incorrect in his travel estimates. This same monarchy who turned him down became his lifeline six years later. Columbus held fast.

Fear of rejection lurks over us all! Our thoughts can paralyze us. We must not tie our self-worth to other people's approval. We need to silence the thoughts of rejection with biblical truth. Scripture says, "Fear of man will prove to be a snare, but whoever trusts in the LORD is kept safe" (Proverbs 29:25). We find our assurance in knowing God is in charge and "no good thing does he withhold from those who walk uprightly" (Psalm 84:11, ESV). It is always an individual's own decision whether they desire to give, but it should never stop us from asking. We need to constantly remember our confidence comes from Christ, not the approval of peers.

Failure. Another haunting anxiety is the fear of failure. Jesus addressed this in a story about a man and his three servants in Matthew 25. The man left on journey and put the servants in charge of his money. When the man returned, the first and second servants had doubled their money, but the third buried his money for fear of losing it. The servant said, "Master ... I knew that you are a hard man, harvesting where you have not sown and gathering where you have not scattered seed. So I was afraid and went out and hid your gold in the ground" (Matthew 25:24-25). The master rebukes him for his laziness, saying, "You wicked, lazy servant! So you knew that I harvest where I have not sown and gather where I have not scattered seed? Well then, you should have put my money on deposit with the bankers, so that when I returned I would have received it back with interest" (vv. 26-27). In the parable, the servant's issue was not that he hadn't received any talents but that he had an improper view of the master. He grumbles that the master requires too much of him, and punishes him for what he cannot help. The master, on the other hand, knows the servant's capabilities and gave him what he was able to handle. Though the anxiety of failing may be close, it should never derail us. We are reminded, "The righteous falls seven times and rises again" (Proverbs 24:16, ESV). In working through anxiety, we realize our worst fear shouldn't be failing, but succeeding at things that are not important.

Debt. Can I really ask people for money, then use it for school loans? Is this wrong? Ministries handle financial support the same as any job handles income. The individual raises support, then receives a monthly paycheck. With your income, it would not be wrong to factor in paying off debt. The amount of your support goal will be drastically different if you have $20,000 in debt versus $100,000. Simply factor your monthly payment into your budget and move forward. Debt should not disqualify anyone from ministry, but if the debt is significant, they may be advised to reduce it before raising support.

Though all of these issues are legitimate, they are not the core issue. These are what we *feel* are the issues, but we need to dig a little deeper.

WHAT WE NEED

After counseling hundreds of young adults, the three core concepts I have observed in support raising are training, accountability, and a proper view of God.[1]

Training: This is commonly overlooked but easy to access. Some think since they have raised money for a short-term trip they can jump into raising monthly support. They can, but they still need training.

I read a book on some of the best marathon runners in the world, the Tarahumara.[2] The Tarahumara are a superathletic tribe in Mexico who can easily run over three hundred miles with little to no effort! That's ten marathons in a row. When I read the book, I had never run over three miles. After reading it, I decided to run a full marathon. After all, 26.2 miles seemed like a walk in the park compared to three hundred. So I laced up my shoes and set out. My goal was to run until I could not run anymore. I started with the wind at my back and music in my ears. After what felt like an hour, my legs started shaking. Feeling spent, I looked to see how far I had run: 1.5 miles. Are you kidding me? I was distraught. I learned a hard lesson that day. Just because I know about marathon runners doesn't mean I am one. I needed training.

When you begin raising support you may know how to send letters or make phone calls, but there is so much more. No one would walk into a new job and bypass all instructions and training. Whether it is a day, a week, or a month of training, we need to know the most effective ways of raising support. To get started with support raising, check into the incredible resources provided by ministries such as Support Raising Solutions.[3]

Seek Accountability: This comes in close behind training. When we have goals and standards yet no accountability, we will fail. An accountability mentor brings refreshment and counsel. This is the main reason I made it to full support. They would listen to my sob stories and respond with Scripture, encouragement, and sometimes hard truth. I submitted a weekly report of all the letters sent, phone calls made, support meetings set up, and meetings attained. All this accountability kept me on task toward my goal. If you intend to raise support you must have someone walk with you.

Melissa was joining a ministry and knew she would need to raise support. At first she was burdened in light of the stories she heard. There were people in the ministry who had been raising support for over two years and had barely crossed the halfway mark. Foreseeing the pitfalls, Melissa took the initiative to get extra training and recruited people to hold her accountable. In the end Melissa said,

> I love support raising! Although it wasn't always easy, as I was working full-time and taking a class, as well as the "normal life" roles I have. I stayed busy making phone calls and appointments to ask people face to face to be a part of my financial partnership team and a part of what God is doing. It was such a blessing for me to cast a vision for missions. It's so neat to see God at work in others' lives and to see their heart grow for Him. I set my target goal of four months to be fully funded and it happened! God provided, but not without effort on my part.

Melissa understood where God guides He provides. She sought to be a good steward of her time and the investments made in her.

Training and accountability are not all you need. Some need a new view of God.

Proper View of God: I am convinced the biggest obstacle

to support raising is having an improper view of God. He is the Creator. He places the stars where He desires and tells the rivers where to flow. Yet, in all of this grandness, He desires to take care of us. Matthew tells us God feeds the birds and clothes the grass and says, "Are you not much more valuable than they?" (6:26). He provides for us because He loves us. As the psalmist says, "Come and see what God has done, his awesome deeds for mankind!" (Psalm 66:5).

God has called us. He is a loving Father. When you ask Him for provision, He will not give you something insufficient (see Matthew 7:9-11). Indeed, we must all hold fast to God no matter what line of work we are in.

HOLD THE ROPE

In the 1780s, pioneer missionary William Carey started seeing the world through a new lens. As he read the Bible, he realized God's passion for all nations; however, the climate of Carey's time was anything but accepting of missions. By gathering data, Carey was able to chart the world's religions and populations on a handmade map. One Sunday, Carey rose to plead with a group to consider God's passion for the nations. In response, one pastor stated, "If God wants to convert the heathen, He can do it without your help or mine."[4] Unwavering, Carey set his mind on taking the gospel where it wasn't: India. While deliberating with friends on who would go rescue the gold mine of souls in India, Carey looked at them and declared, "I will go down, if you will hold the rope."[5] Carey knew he would need a team of givers to hold fast in the mission of reaching India. One of his friends, John Ryland, wrote that Carey "took an oath from each of us, at the mouth of the pit ...

that 'while we lived, we should never let go of the rope.'"[6] His friends faithfully held the rope to the end of Carey's days. Without exception, we should all be involved in God's mission, whether going or sending. We all play a role in the Great Commission. The question is, do you have a rope?

ENDNOTES

1. In observing these concepts, I also consulted with Steve Shadrach, executive director of Support Raising Solutions, for insight into obstacles and concepts of successful support raising.

2. Christopher McDougall, *Born to Run: A Hidden Tribe, Superathletes, and the Greatest Race the World Has Never Seen* (New York: Knopf, 2009).

3. Steve Shadrach's Support Raising Solutions is a ministry that has trained thousands of individuals to raise their support. To learn more, visit http://supportraisingsolutions.org/.

4. Reportedly said by John Ryland Sr., Marc A. Jolley, and John D. Pierce, eds., *Distinctively Baptist Essays on Baptist History* (Macon, GA: Mercer University Press, 2005), 11.

5. John Piper, *Andrew Fuller* (Minneapolis, MN: Desiring God Foundation, 2012), 5.

6. Piper, *Andrew Fuller*, 5.

Chapter Eleven

The Laborers Are Few
The Need

Few know the names Brad and Beth Buser, but they are one of the most influential couples I have ever met. In his early years Brad was touted as one of the best up-and-coming young surfers in California. His senior year of high school, he had a serious conversion after hearing the gospel from a local pastor. When Brad turned over his life, he was all in. The old Brad was changing, and his perspective on surfing being his "total life" was a huge part of that change.

After graduation, lots of people encouraged Brad to go pro. Brad had other plans. He wanted to share Jesus with those who had never had a chance to hear the gospel. His parents tried their best to discourage him, but Brad was relentless. During missionary training he met and married Beth. At twenty-three, with two kids, Brad and Beth jumped on a plane and made their way from urban San Diego to Papua New Guinea (PNG). PNG is off the coast of Indonesia and is home to six million people making up over 860 people groups. The Busers were there for one group, the Iteri (pronounced "Iteddi"). After six years of living in a hut and studying the language, Brad was able to share God's story from Creation to Christ. In March of 1986, the first Iteri believed in Christ. Today the Busers are able to pass their torch of leadership to the multiplying Iteri church.

When Brad came back to the US, I met him. I'll never forget one phrase he said: "If you want to do something big for the kingdom of God, get used to saying no to a lot of good opportunities." From experience, the Busers know what it means to hold fast. Every obstacle we have discussed, the Busers have experienced in some form. Still, they would say to this day that being a part of God's mission to reach the nations is the greatest thing they could do. As we have seen, there are many reasons to withdraw, but through joy we hold fast and navigate through.

Just before sending out the disciples, Jesus encouraged them, saying, "The harvest is plentiful, but the laborers are few" (Luke 10:2, ESV). Through many miracles, God is preparing the hearts of people around the world for the arrival of the good news. The fields are ripe for harvest, waiting for someone to reap the fruit. Yet Jesus recognized the scarcity of laborers. The definition of labor is *to strive painstakingly.* One dictionary defined it as "to plod," meaning to proceed in a tediously slow manner. The actual Greek word for labor is *kopos* and primarily denotes "a striking or beating." The vision you get is someone striking a piece of metal over and over and over again, continually doing the same difficult act until the work is done. Simply put, a laborer does the difficult things. This is why there are so few.

Luke 10 continues, "Therefore pray earnestly to the Lord of the harvest to send out laborers into his harvest." (v. 2, ESV). It is in the asking for more laborers that the Lord taps our shoulder, and we realize we are the very answer to that prayer.

Many sailors used to have the phrase "hold fast" tattooed on their hands. Some said the tattoo would help the sailor grip the ropes more securely. The obstacles are waiting to derail us. We fight back by gripping tightly and holding fast to the hope of the end goal—the earth filled with worshippers of Jesus. One day every people group will have representatives worshipping Jesus, and heaven will be filled. The task of testifying to the nations will be finished, and the mission will be no more. We who excuse ourselves from involvement in God's mission will be excusing ourselves from the ultimate blessing of God—to take the gospel to the ends of the earth. Indeed, Jesus is worth holding fast. Enjoy the journey.

Appendix 1

The Stayer

I learned in college the world was closer than I realized. Behind me in line at a coffee shop stood a five-foot bald man wearing a red bathrobe. My college was full of odd people, but this was beyond the usual. As I stared at him, I noticed he wasn't from the US. I also noticed that his bathrobe wasn't a bathrobe. It was a religious robe like the ones worn by monks. So I asked, "Where are you from?" In a thick accent he replied, "Tibet." I was blown away! My only knowledge of Tibet was, well, I knew nothing of Tibet. This guy was the real thing. After talking for a few minutes, I held my hand to give a traditional American farewell, a high five. His face lit up. "That was my first high five," he said. I gave a Tibetan Buddhist monk his first high five. How cool is that?

Today all you have to do is walk down the street to meet someone from a different country. The world is small. With the mandate from Christ and the growing diversity in the world, it is essential that we learn to engage the nations. In the past, we reduced missions to *over there* or *not at all*. But you don't have to cross an ocean to be involved with what God is doing. There is a way to hold fast to the vision no matter your location or vocation. I received a letter from a couple who wrote, "We've been praying about what God wants for our lives. We really feel our hearts are overseas but our bodies are here. We would like to help anyway we can. What are our options?" What would you tell them? There are ways to engage in the task of global missions without quitting your job and moving to the Middle East. We can pray, send, welcome, and mobilize. We are all to be Global Christians no matter where we live.

A Global Christian is someone who knows the truth and need for fulfilling God's unfulfilled global purpose. They realize as a Christian they are responsible to think, act, pray, and believe according to the knowledge of this truth. The Global Christian is involved no matter where God has them. Here is how.

Praying. The most impactful thing anyone can do for the unreached is to pray. In Matthew 9, Jesus was traveling throughout many villages and cities preaching, healing, and teaching. As He traveled His heart was broken for the people. "When he saw the crowds, he had compassion for them.... Then he said to his disciples, 'The harvest is plentiful, but the laborers are few; *therefore pray* earnestly to the Lord of the harvest to send out laborers into his harvest'" (Matthew 9:36-38, ESV, emphasis added). Jesus' response to the lack of laborers was prayer, because God advances the gospel through the prayers of His people.

What would it look like to start praying for the world? JoshuaProject.net is an online resource that posts the most recent facts and prayer needs on all people groups. *Operation World* by Jason Mandryk is a book outlining every country in the world and how to pray for each specifically. A few college girls I knew bought *Operation World*. They met once a week in a dorm and prayed through the countries. The next semester the prayer group grew so large they split in two. The following year all the girls started their own prayer groups. They had a group in every dorm on campus! Prayer aligns our hearts with the mission of God.

Sending. Sending is an integral part of spreading the

gospel. The Global Christian sees money provided by God as a blessing meant for the nations. The sad reality is Americans spend more money on Halloween costumes *for their pets* than on reaching unreached peoples.[1] Being a businessman, teacher, doctor, or factory worker doesn't prevent you from God's mission. Anyone can engage the nations through financially equipping missionaries.

Giving financially can be extremely difficult for people on a tight budget or full-time students. Julie wanted to give, but she always felt strapped for cash. By simply reviewing her spending, Julie realized she was buying seven dollars' worth of coffee every day. She had no idea! As a result, she curbed her caffeine by making coffee at home and giving the rest away.

Sending isn't just supporting a missionary or giving to your local church. It can include housing a missionary on furlough, organizing logistical support, or orchestrating e-mails, letters, or packages. Being a sender enlarges our heart for the nations. Senders play a crucial role.

Welcoming. Over forty times in the Old Testament, God commands to care for the foreigner residing in the country. "The foreigner residing among you must be treated as your native-born. Love them as yourself, for you were foreigners in Egypt. I am the LORD your God" (Leviticus 19:34). "He defends the cause of the fatherless and the widow, and loves the foreigner residing among you, giving them food and clothing. And you are to love those who are foreigners, for you yourself were foreigners in Egypt" (Deuteronomy 10:18-19). Jesus modeled this by reaching out to different nations. As He was ministering He came upon a Samaritan woman at a well (see John 4:7-30). His disciples were shocked to see Jesus talking with her, because the Jews and the Samaritans had a long history of conflict. Jesus put aside custom and offered her healing. The disciples were stunned. They couldn't believe it! Jesus didn't stop there. He continually reached out to foreigners throughout His ministry, like the Canaanite woman (see Matthew 15:21-28). She came to Jesus and begged Him to heal her daughter. His disciples said, "Send her away, for she keeps crying out after us." Jesus wanted to see her. He marveled at the faith of this woman and granted her request to heal her daughter. Jesus' love for the foreigner permeated His ministry. The feeding of the four thousand (see Mark 8) and the healing of the demon-possessed men at the Gadarenes (see Matthew 8) are examples. He didn't just watch them. He talked to them, touched them, healed them, and died for them. The foreigner has always been close to the Lord's heart; therefore, they should be close to ours.

America is home to nearly 800,000 internationals from 200 nations.[2] Most of these are studying in our colleges. Even more compelling, eight of the top ten countries studying in the US are from the 10/40 Window.[3] These countries have sent their best and brightest to get an education. Walking onto a college campus, you can meet with future politicians and business owners, and influence the influentials of the next generation. The most strategic thing you can do might be to open your home. What would it look like to cook them dinner, drive them to the grocery store, or go watch a movie?

For missionaries it's difficult to get into some countries, but *welcoming* reverses those hardships. While in Los Angeles, my friend met a Saudi Arabian who was vacationing with his family. For an hour they talked about the Bible, the Quran, and Jesus. This was the first, and most likely the only, time he would ever hear the gospel. The melting pot of America provides amazing opportunities to engage the nations. You don't have to raise support, you don't have to get a passport, and you don't have to learn a new language. What an incredible opportunity in today's world.

Mobilizing. A mobilizer has a passion for the world and a passion to pass it on. Everyone is a mobilizer to something. For many it's mobilizing to clothes, music, or restaurants. But the Global Christian has a passion to get others engaged in God's mission. Habakkuk 2:2 says, "Record the vision and inscribe it on tablets, that the one who reads it may run" (NASB). Habakkuk was told by God to write down his vision so others would respond. This is the vision mobilizers have. At the core of the mobilizer is a desire to ignite a passion in the hearts of others.

I used to think mobilizers were only powerful, effective speakers who spoke to thousands of people every year. I was wrong. Mobilizers are equally effective whether one-on-one or in small-group settings. There are mobilizers who do well in large groups, but some of the most effective mobilization happens on a small scale, sometimes as simple as walking through God's Word with another. Regardless of the platform, the mobilizer beats the drum of reaching the unreached.

Praying, sending, welcoming, and mobilizing are habits Christians do in obedient response to God's passion. They are not just a single role. All can be cultivated. A good challenge for any believer would be to begin with the one that scares you the most. It has nothing to do with our giftings or location. It has everything to do with our passion to make God known where He isn't. We all should be Global Christians whether we are goers or stayers. Find your role and walk in it!

ENDNOTES

1. "General Statistics: Money and Missions," The Traveling Team, accessed March 29, 2013, http://www.thetravelingteam.org/stats.

2. Institute of International Education, "International Student Totals by Place of Origin, 2009/10 - 2010/11," *Open Doors Report on International Educational Exchange*, 2011, http://www.iie.org/opendoors.

3. Institute of International Education, "International Student Totals," http://www.iie.org/opendoors.

Appendix 2

Finding an Agency

by Todd Ahrend and Josh Cooper

We have attended conferences where many mission agencies were represented. They typically have incredible booths equipped with the latest attention grabbers—Frisbees, bumper stickers, globes, and candy. Those who come to the conference looking for an agency are completely overwhelmed. If one doesn't know what they're looking for, they run the risk of committing to the agency with the most exciting booth or the brochure with the best graphics.

We highly encourage going with an agency, but the differences between agencies can be extreme. With over four thousand mission agencies and a multitude of church-sending groups, there are all types of ways to get where you want to go. Mission agencies and churches offer accountability and support. With agencies, you have a team of people working behind the scenes who help with finances, transportation and logistics, prayer support, insurance, and taxes. Ultimately there will always be someone you can turn to regardless of the need.

Two centuries ago, taking a business to the Middle East was nearly impossible. Today, reaching the world through business, medicine, or nearly any given skill set has become a forte of many agencies. Ministries are covering nearly every facet of the mission field, adapting to the needs of the world. For those who choose to go with an agency the difficulty begins with finding the right one.

SAYING "I DO"

It's easy to be overwhelmed with all the details. You may not even know where to start. Deciding on an agency is a lot like dating; you need to get to know the person, but you also need to know yourself. Here are some helpful questions to think through when choosing a mission agency.

What's your vision? This should be one of the first questions you ask. When you think about going overseas, what comes to your mind? Is it a people, a place, a job, or a religious group? Most people who go overseas generally have an initial idea of who, where, or what they want to do. It's a vague God-given passion in the core that drives you to the point of going overseas. Answering this question will drastically narrow down agencies.

Where does the agency serve? Some agencies can be whittled down because of their location. Some are based on religious areas, others geographic areas. Do you want your agency to only focus on your part of the world, or are you open to them being more diverse?

What are the strategies? If your vision is to work with orphans, it would be easy to figure out whether a particular ministry has a job for you. You may agree on a country and you may agree on a people, but you may be bent toward social-justice issues while the agency primarily leans toward evangelism. The difference is huge. Most agencies will have a purpose statement about the goal of the ministry and the means of accomplishing it. There will be days when living in a foreign land will be challenging. Finding your niche and vision before crossing the culture will enable you to push through and strive for continued effectiveness in ministry.

What's the average day like? A typical day on the mission field can look extremely different from a typical day in the US. When learning more about the agency, you need to ask about what a day on the field entails. Sometimes this is easily explained. Other times it's not. One group may have an established program and role you fill. Another may be starting something where no one has gone before. In this case, flexibility is essential to navigate the unknowns. A good question to ask yourself is, "Am I in need of structure and details, or am I spontaneous and flexible?"

On-field realities differ greatly based on personnel. Do you work better with a team or as an individual? Who will you report to? Will you be working with Americans only or people from other countries?

How am I evaluated? Evaluation can often be relative in ministry, but it is vital for the continuation of a ministry. Depending on the organization's platform and individual roles, the evaluation may vary significantly. Do they look at hourly requirements, or are they task-oriented? Which do you work better with?

How will my family be incorporated? Family life can be an obstacle that keeps missionaries out of the field. Are both husband and wife required to do ministry? Who will take care of and educate children? How often do you get to return to your homeland? What emotional or psychological support system does the agency offer? It is important to understand how agencies view the role of the spouse and children.

What is their finance system like? Money issues can tear groups apart. It's essential to learn the ins and outs of the financial system set up by the organization. Where does a missionary's salary come from? Is support raising necessary, or is income covered organizationally? Are there benefits and medical insurance provided? Who is responsible for mailing donation receipts? What is the view on being fully funded?

How much Bible do I need? Theological training has changed since the birth of American missions. In the past, it was required that all missionaries go to seminary. Today, you can go without ever stepping foot in a Christian school. Some agencies do their own training which must be completed before going. Some have required classes everyone takes, either before joining or within a few years. Others require theological degrees. Of the larger agencies, many have trimmed back their theological views to encompass more people. This is good for getting missionaries to the field, but could be a source of conflict while overseas. Charismatic or conservative? Evangelism or social justice? Thinking through your theological beliefs needs to happen sooner rather than later to help with team dynamics and ministry.

The first American missionaries were sailing to India when they hit a dissension on infant baptism.[1] Half the group thought it should be done, the other group said no. By the time they arrived in India, the two groups were split. Though they remained friends they decided their teams were better separate rather than together. Similar problems exist today.

Most agencies will have either a denominational stance or a set of beliefs that are their core values. Learning these will help decide if you are a good fit. You will have many other questions along the way. Rob Antonucci, former missionary to the Muslim world, has thought through important issues to consider when trying to find the right mission agency for you:

1. Check out their promotional literature and brochures. Remember, this type of literature is only introductory; you need to ask further questions. Listen to their catchphrases and how they define them; for example, *church planting, unreached, strategic, teams.*

2. Are they working among the unreached? What do they mean by this term? When they say there are no churches do they mean of their denomination? Does unreached mean they work among nonbelievers, or among those who don't go to the local church? Many are surprised when they get to their "unreached" area and find many workers doing ministry among a multitude of churches.

3.* Does the mission agency believe in closure, that is, finishing their work and moving on to new areas?

4.* What are their statistics? What is the source of information? Is it verifiable? After a mistruth is repeated many times it tends to become accepted as fact. Use caution; some statistics are hypothetical and are designed for high impact only.

5.* Do they use glory stories? All mission agencies are guilty of some misuse of stories of incredible workings of God in a place. Example: "One thousand people converted in one day in country X." Look beneath the surface, get past the headlines, and look for details. Remember that glory stories alone don't necessarily give an accurate picture of what life is like in a particular ministry.

6. How willing is an agency to work with your local church? Is your church going to take an active part in the ministry?*

(*These subjects may be more appropriate for someone looking to go long-term and are not necessarily of interest to the short-term missionary.)

Working through these questions with a mission agency will greatly ease the pain of moving to a new culture, a new country, and smooth potential rough roads.

MISSIONS AGENCIES

There are thousands of agencies to choose from. Not every agency will be right for you. Narrowing down the choices can help with effectiveness in your work overseas and with your satisfaction in ministry. Here is a list to start your search:

Café 1040 – cafe1040.com
Café 10/40 is an intense three-month experiential training program inside the 10/40 Window for Christian college students. Learn the cultural and strategic side to missions, as well as how to live and minister in the hardest places.

CEO Global – ceoglobal.org
CEO Global is an educational nonprofit that was invited to operate officially in China to train servant leaders of integrity among Chinese university students. They are working to see a new generation of leaders raised up who will transform China and the world.

Chosen People Ministries – chosenpeople.com
Do you have a heart for Jewish people? Chosen People has outreaches to Jewish people in Chicago, New York, and Israel, which include evangelism, discipleship, publications, and benevolence. Imagine two weeks or two months in Israel—not only walking in the footsteps of Jesus but sharing the gospel too!

ELIC – elic.org
ELIC invests in the lives of teenagers in Asia through conversational English teaching, high-energy games, sports, and cultural activities. ELIC can train you how to teach conversational English and have a ministry while you do it. Go with them for two months to two years in China, Mongolia, Vietnam, Laos, Cambodia, or Myanmar.

Mission to Unreached Peoples – mup.org
MUP seeks to be catalysts in starting movements of rapidly reproducing disciples and churches among the least-reached people groups in the world. They place small teams throughout Asia to love the people, learn their language and culture, and share Jesus.

Pioneers – pioneers.org
Their name says it all: total focus on the unreached. Join a team of college students for two, six, or eight weeks over the summer and live in an unreached people group. Pioneers wants to take your passions and give them a road to run on to reach the nations for Jesus.

South America Mission – southamericamission.org
Do you have a heart for South America? South America Mission is building God's kingdom by living in response to the gospel of grace through short- and long-term ministry in Colombia, Bolivia, Peru, Brazil, Paraguay, and Argentina. Their vision is to make God famous through redeemed lives, beautiful churches, and transformed communities.

Veritas – veritasabroad.com
The mission of Veritas Christian Study Abroad is to provide college-level study-abroad programs at host universities while helping students develop as missions-minded Christian leaders. Students who study on a Veritas program will have opportunities to work with local missionaries while they earn college credit toward their degree.

Avant – avantministries.org
Ever wonder what church planting looks like? Avant has a five-year church-planting cycle that is growing the church rapidly among the unreached. Spend a summer learning from them and assisting as they evangelize and disciple on the front lines.

GoCorps – gocorps.org
What's your next step after graduation? Use your major overseas with GoCorps, an on-ramp to multiple organizations to help you find a place you can serve with a strategic, long-term project. All positions are for two years, are among the least-reached and global poor, and all goers receive $5,000 in student loan forgiveness.

International Mission Board – thetask.org
IMB's desire is to lead Southern Baptists to be on mission with God to bring all the peoples of the world to saving faith in Jesus Christ. IMB is connecting the current generation with the world in relational and strategic ways. Whether college-age or married with children, the IMB can help connect you to finish the task.

International Teams – iteams.org/go
Looking for an integrated approach that blends compassion and evangelism in the context of international community development? Check out ITeams. Join teams around the world serving in particular areas of need among the poor, refugees, enslaved, and those seeking the Kingdom. ITeams brings people together to help the oppressed.

MECO – aboutmeco.org
MECO (Middle East Christian Outreach) is a group with a heart for the Middle East that is united in vision for Middle Eastern churches to engage in effective mission. They are determined to stay around for the long term to embody the love of Christ in a culturally sensitive way.

New Tribes Mission – ntm.org
These guys only go to the tribal world. With their Interface program, you spend a summer in Papua New Guinea and learn to share the gospel with tribal people while living among them. What a great six-week experience!

NEXT Worldwide – nextworldwide.org
NEXT Worldwide exists to radically transform the way you see the mission of God in your life. When you go with

NEXT on a short-term trip, you work alongside a national church planter to help establish a local church in an area with little or no gospel witness. Through daily practical leadership training and local community engagement, you'll have a powerful experience that will propel you to a lifetime of kingdom service both at home and around the world.

OMF International – omf.org

Interested in Asia? OMF (formerly China Inland Mission and Overseas Missionary Fellowship) has it all. From baking to teaching, business to sports, this group wants to use your motivations, skills, and degree to plug into the pipeline of reaching Asia. Go for two weeks to six months, or a lifetime. For over 150 years OMF has been exhibiting their passion, "Heart for Asia. Hope for billions."

ReachGlobal – goreachglobal.org

ReachGlobal seeks to develop, empower, and release local leaders to touch their cultures holistically and multiply healthy kingdom communities among all peoples. Use the gifts and strengths God has given you to make a difference.

Teach Overseas – teachoverseas.org

The heart of Teach Overseas is Christlike service through excellent teaching. By serving as a conversational English teacher you can gain access to closed countries while meeting real needs in a practical way. Teachers receive excellent pre-field training and in-field support. Visit their website to find out how you can share Christ's love through teaching for a summer or for a full school year.

TEAM – teamworld.org

The purpose of TEAM (The Evangelical Alliance Mission) is to help churches send missionaries to establish reproducing churches among the nations. For over a century, they have sought to accomplish this through community health, community development, leadership training, education, English teaching, and various technical and professional services.

TWR – twr.org

Speaking fluently in more than 230 languages and dialects, TWR (Trans World Radio) joins international partners and local churches in using high-powered radio, Internet streaming, and face-to-face contact to have a lasting gospel impact around the world. TWR needs missions-minded people in overseas locations like Singapore, Guam, Austria, South Africa, or even the Caribbean. Whether you're an engineer, an accountant, an info techie, a retiree, or someone in between, TWR offers opportunities to use your skills to further God's kingdom.

United World Mission – uwm.org

United World Mission has a "mission apprenticeship" program called Expedition237. Participants serve overseas for two years, building relationships, understanding culture, learning a new language, and working in a team with others to make Christ known. Receive ongoing training and mentoring from a community of long-term missionaries while serving together.

East-West Ministries International – eastwest.org
Taking resources from the West to equip the East, this
organization uses every facet of society to take the gospel to
and establish the church in the most spiritually dark places
on earth. They focus on building and mobilizing the church
by encouraging and empowering nationals to spread the
gospel to create a self-sustaining ministry.

Operation Mobilisation – om.org
OM is serving around the world, seeking to demonstrate
and proclaim the love of God. By adapting to each location,
OM tries to find the best way to share the gospel using
literature, the creative arts, friendship, Bible studies, media,
relief work, and development. Join them for one week to
two years in transforming lives and communities.

Radius International – radiusinternational.org
Radius International is a training center that prepares
pioneer cross-cultural church planters by giving them
the understanding and information (know), skills and
competencies (do), and character qualities (be) necessary
to be successful cross-cultural church planters among
unreached people groups.

Frontiers – frontiers.org
Frontiers sends teams of ordinary people for short-term
and long-term service to the communities of the Muslim
world. They serve in businesses, community development,
and other service capacities to help reach those in need.
This is a unique organization built in community, sent by
communities (fellowships and churches), and living for
communities (Muslim peoples).

CRU Global Missions - cruoncampus.org/go/international/ CRU is building real relationships and experiencing life in another country while affecting the course of history by sharing Jesus' love with future leaders on college campuses around the world. CRU Summer Projects give a taste of international, cross-cultural ministry for two to six weeks. Study Abroad with CRU is a unique opportunity to be part of helping spiritual movements grow during semester, while potentially earning school credit. CRU STINT is one or two years of the campus ministry internship program at an international university location.

ENDNOTES

1. Courtney Anderson, *To the Golden Shore: The Life of Adoniram Judson* (Valley Forge, PA: Judson Press, 1987), 127.
2. Todd Ahrend, *The Ten Modules* (Conway, AR: The Traveling Team, 2002), 75–76.

To order more copies of *Hold Fast*,
visit www.givingtons.com.

You may also contact Book Villages,
www.bookvillages.com.

You may also visit www.HoldFastBook.com

To book this author for speaking, e-mail:
schedule@thetravelingteam.org